# Rebels, Poets, and Mystics

## Challenging the Truth of a Spiritual Life

by
Daniel Burow

ISBN: 978-1-57579-388-7

Library of Congress Control Number: 2008936694

PUBLISHED BY MAIEUTIC PUBLISHING
Sioux Falls, South Dakota
2008

*Printed in the United States of America*

PINE HILL PRESS
4000 West 57th Street
Sioux Falls, SD 57106

*Better worlds (I suggest) are born, not made;*
*and their birthdays are the birthdays of individuals.*
*Let us pray always for individuals; never for worlds.*
E.E. Cummings, <u>Six Nonlectures</u>

# Dedication

For the doubters, heretics, rebels and outlaws. Those who make
the mistakes and say the words necessary to be who they are.

# Acknowledgments

There are ideas, stories and even sentences in this book you may have heard or seen before. This material is not mine nor is it Fr. Frahms'. It has lived in the hearts of countless people and traditions for thousands of years. I am, in truth, just repeating what others have repeated before.

I gratefully acknowledge:
My editor Doug Morano for his interest and talent.
Tom Gilbert for his constant time, encouragement
and critical thoughts.
Jan Hodge for his direction and guidance.

# Table of Contents

**Part One:**
Introduction: Real Teachers and the Hazards of Freedom ................................... 1

Chapter One:
What's Your Distance From God? ................................................................. 9

Chapter Two:
Another Kind of Freedom ......................................................................... 13

Chapter Three:
The Foundation of Love ............................................................................ 21

Chapter Four:
Witnessing a Life ..................................................................................... 25

Chapter Five:
Witnessing a Death ................................................................................. 35

Chapter Six:
When the Student is Ready ....................................................................... 43

Chapter Seven:
The Teacher will Come ............................................................................. 51

**Part Two:**
The Tool Box ........................................................................................... 71

Chapter Eight:
Fr. Frahm's Presence ............................................................................... 73

Chapter Nine:
A Spiritual Life ........................................................................................ 79

Chapter Ten:
**Christianity and Faith** ........................................................... 91

Chapter Eleven:
**Religion** .................................................................................. 101

Chapter Twelve:
**Not Freedom From, but Freedom To** ..................................... 109

Chapter Thirteen:
**Silent Laughter** ..................................................................... 115

Chapter Fourteen:
**Free Love** ............................................................................... 121

Chapter Fifteen:
**Judgment, a Cautionary Tale** ................................................ 127

Chapter Sixteen:
**The Sound of Death** .............................................................. 135

Chapter Seventeen:
**Prayer and Other Forms of Hypocrisy** ................................. 145

Chapter Eighteen:
**I Play, Therefore I Am** ........................................................... 151

Chapter Nineteen:
**Nature** .................................................................................... 157

Chapter Twenty:
**This Life** ................................................................................ 163

Afterward

Biography of Fr. Frahm

About the Author

Bibliography

# Part One

# Introduction

*Four men went to an orchard. Ben Azai looked inside and lost his mind: Ben Soma looked inside and died. Elisha Ben Avuya looked and converted to Paganism (the Talmud calls him Acher – "other" – the Gentile). Only Rabbi Akiva came out whole, yet even then the angels wished to push him but God said: "Leave the old one alone as he is worthy of my honor."*

(Hagiga 14)

We live our lives in exile. If you've spent any time in solitude or experienced any real pain you probably already know this. And you've probably tried to do something about it. Each of us desires a connection to something larger than our isolated individual lives. From substance use to depression, from orthodoxy to evangelical, from employment to consumerism all of us are trying to connect to something that removes our sense of exile, if even for a moment. A smaller group of us have moved beyond yearning for mere connection and are actively searching for a real spiritual life. We are driven toward an existence that allows us to feel an actual connection to whatever is Divine in the universe. Never before has our society seen such a large group of people openly searching for a felt sense of connection to God.

Many of us wander into any orchard that shows promise. From this Church to that religion and this group to that workshop we travel hoping for a connection to God that will relieve our sense of exile and the enormous feeling of isolation and pain that accompanies it. We see a new orchard and we look in, only to discover that despite all the promises, God is nowhere to be found.

Yet, we look. Every day we search the places where we think God might be. All this effort and most of us still find nothing, which leads us most often to sadness and hopelessness. Then one day, if you're lucky, you realize that you can go looking for God all you like and all you'll ever really find is your own reflection. This is no accident. If you are honestly looking for God you will find him in the only place he could ever be - inside the heart of a human being.

Out there among us are old ones that have looked into the orchard and came out whole. They looked deep inside themselves and were not destroyed by the process. All of them have something to say, it depends very much on whether they believe you are ready to hear it. If they think you're not they will usually stay silent and you'll never know what they've seen. But if they believe you might be ready, what they show you will change your world forever.

This is a story about finding an old one who went into the orchard and came out whole. Fr. Gary Frahm was my teacher and he became my best friend. Long before I met him I had looked into the orchard myself and I did not come out whole. What I saw was an emptiness that consumed the next fifteen years of my life.

I made my living as a psychologist and I had studied human behavior for almost a decade. I spent countless hours and tens of thousands of dollars learning to help people cope with the suffering and difficulties of everyday life. After all this training, I can't honestly say that my success was anything more than moderate. The people who came to work with me left still hurting, lost and alone. This is no surprise as I spent most of my time feeling lost and alone myself. And like them, my most frequent therapeutic success was the occasional new and improved method for keeping my problems at a distance for a day or two.

Then one dark Tuesday night, I met a man with a completely different understanding of what it is to be a human being. This man was Fr. Gary Frahm, a retired Episcopalian Priest and poet who took my rigid, self-involved view of what was real and poked holes in it until nothing remained. And when nothing was all I had, I was finally able to see something new. Fr. Frahm was the rarest of creatures: a true spiritual teacher who was able to invite those around him into a world without boundaries, into a world that was more real than any I had ever known.

When asked certain questions about who or what he was, Fr. Frahm would identify himself as a contemplative. Once, when speaking to a group of students about the contemplative life, Fr. Frahm described this different reality to them. "Contemplatives are people who, really awake to the present, see the hollowness of success, the emptiness of achievements, the vanity and nothingness of human striving: a vision which, surprisingly, leads them not to pessimism and despair but to excitement and freedom. And, occasionally, one of them strays in the wrong stable yard and mounts a steed with vast white wings to go soaring out above the bottomless abyss, all the while stretching to embrace and kiss the Mystery."

Every day, we encounter new people, places and things that invite us to share some of who we are. Most of these meetings dwindle away to nothing all too quickly. Some take root and become lasting relationships. A handful of these relationships, which are beautiful and filled with discovery, become something more. A precious one or two of these however, will be extraordinary events so far beyond words like friendship, love, or wonder that they leave a permanent mark on our lives. We are marked by what we learn about who we actually are, and what is truly real.

All of our significant relationships mark us in some small way, but that rare one or two leave a hole in our psyche that we can't pretend isn't there. These marks are the beginning of a journey that we can neither predict nor control. It is this journey(s) that contains our only opportunity for real growth in this life. For human beings, true growth always lies beyond the narrow confines of what we think about ourselves, our world and God. Only when all this is left behind are we free to move toward the unknown in ourselves, our world and our God.

Think about the people in your life who left a mark on you. Bring the faces and the memories into your mind, and just sit with them for awhile. Now I would like to ask you a question.

*Who was it that set you free?*

Many things might come into your mind. Take some time to follow your thoughts. Allow this to expand, develop, and add depth to the question. Now, ask yourself again.

*Who was it that set you free?*

I'm talking about an amazing moment, or moments where you were able to safely doubt who you are and what you know. With this doubt came a grace that loosened your grip on certainty and allowed you to be a larger and/or wiser human being. Once cramped habits or automatic responses suddenly had enough space to slow, stop, and even turn around to take a new direction. Inside this larger space you became something softer and easier in the world. What was your moment of freedom like? What was it about you that changed? More importantly however, who helped you?

Most of us can find a few examples of being set free by what some significant person did or said. Maybe you carry memories of a touch that freed you from pain or isolation. You may also remember phrases like "It's okay" that released you from the burden of a particular moment or event. It takes very little effort in most instances to find an example or two of this freedom within your own life.

I ask who helped you because human beings don't seem to have the ability to free themselves from the lives and worlds they create. I have considered, and still do on certain days, that the sheer inertia of the universe doesn't allow us the time and space we need to free ourselves. It either drags us behind it or we spend all our time and energy resisting its motion. It's more likely, however, that the human mind just won't let go of the reality it carries. It can't let go. The fear of the unknown is overwhelming. If your mind won't let go, the universe won't either, and you will remain stuck right where you are.

Whatever the reason, it is rare for us to change anything in our small worlds, let alone anything within ourselves. We spend most of our time working to become a more sophisticated and well-defended version of what we were yesterday. To our cost, however, this is neither growth nor change. It is ironic that we spend so much time working to change some part of who we are when it is only freedom from this "who" that will allow us to step away from what we think we are and move closer to what is real. But this business of freedom is complicated, and for most of us it requires a teacher. It is only in relationship with a real teacher that the first steps of freedom can be taken.

Many people tell me that they have never encountered a spiritual teacher, but I doubt this is true. If we are even moderately aware of our surroundings, the universe consistently offers us new teachers. It is more likely that our teachers come and we don't recognize them, or worse, we reject them outright believing they have nothing to offer us. But if you can let go of your need to be who you are for even a moment, and the stars are aligned just right, something amazing might happen. You and a spiritual teacher might discover each other, and together you may become more human than either of you had been in the past. This moment and the initial ability to doubt who you are and what is real are the first ingredients of what will become freedom.

I had never sought out a teacher, let alone the first one I saw clearly. Fr. Gary Frahm found me, or I found him, in the most unlikely of places - a small apartment on Ridge Avenue in Sioux City, Iowa. This is important to note, because it seems to me that the most unlikely place is where real teachers are almost always found. It's been my observation that the more someone suggests they are a spiritual teacher the less they have to teach. That being said, I must admit I did nothing to deserve such a relationship and, in fact, I had always tended to reject anything that even resembled a teacher.

Nevertheless, Fr. Frahm invited me into the unknown and for some reason, I went. Now, many years later, I am the caretaker of the memory of a man who was extraordinary. He was extraordinary because he was entirely free. His freedom was not some petty "freedom from this" or "freedom from that." Fr. Frahm, like all spiritual teachers, possessed the most important of all freedoms...spiritual freedom...and this freedom, as he liked to say, is a "freedom to."

So what is spiritual freedom? In its simplest form it is the discovery of the un-reality of everything but the divine. It is the practice of releasing everything that prevents you from being tangibly present with God right this moment. To be spiritually free is to let go of the self you think you are and the world you think you live in and find that God is all that remains.

Learning about spiritual freedom is a challenging task and if you are going to proceed further there is one thing you need to be clear about. First and foremost, you cannot mistake what I tell you for a fact or worse yet for a truth. If you are seeking freedom, you can't mistake what anyone tells you for fact, or truth. This is the paradox of searching for spiritual freedom. Facts, truths, and beliefs can, and often do, make our world less spiritually free. But we like them because they provide safety and certainty, and therefore we are driven to build them out of whatever bits and pieces we have available. In an effort to help you negotiate this challenge, and several others, I want to address a few more things before we begin.

First, this book is a product of my journey, and my mistakes. The ideas I share with you arise out of my experience and my perception. It's important for you to hold the notion that what you do with the ideas that follow has to be your choice. I will offer you ideas and lessons. You need to sit with them and decide what they mean. Neither I, nor anyone else, can tell you about your spiritual life. Fr. Frahm once said to me that religion has about as much to do with spirituality as my clothes have to do with my digestion. This seemed simple at the time, but he didn't tell me how to think and feel about it. It was my job to work that out.

Whatever your response to what follows, it is my hope that you think about what you read. Contemplate it. Try it out. Without cultivating and then owning your experience, freedom of any kind is impossible. No one can tell you what it is or give you the directions to obtain it. It is my hope that you do not just accept what you read here or anywhere else, but that you think it through, change it around, and make it larger. Fr. Frahm told me that people didn't have to be right in their spirituality, just honest. If you do this, whatever your answer is will be the right one...for now.

Secondly, you should know that words are not the best way to teach people about spiritual freedom. If your spiritual teachings are built on words you need to monitor your students every second and ultimately do their thinking for them, because it is likely they heard less of what you said and more of what they already thought and believed to be correct. When we are lucky enough to receive a genuine spiritual lesson, we frequently hear in it only what makes us comfortable and not what was actually offered.

Fr. Frahm was suspicious of words because he knew that when you are working with freedom, particularly spiritual freedom, you are working with boundaries. The largest and most prolific boundary in spiritual development is language. Words suggest the very thing that opposes real spiritual freedom. Every word you use is a symbol of a relatively discrete idea or concept. Words are eager to trick you into believing that ideas, places, people and things are clearly separate, finite, and unique. Words suggest to you that for every hot there is an opposite and opposed cold. For every up there should be a down. Every word we use constructs and reinforces the boundary between that thing and every other thing.

If I say the word "me" it automatically separates "me" from "you." If I remark that I will do something today, your mind compulsively calculates what that has to do with yesterday and tomorrow. No matter what is said: sky/earth, mine/yours, human/animal and so on forever, these words serve to separate everything from every other thing. Every word draws finite boundaries that are automatic, unconscious, and for the most part concrete. If it exists in your mind it exists everywhere.

Each boundary is a potential battle line that requires us to view its two poles as mostly irreconcilable. The more invested we are in the boundary the more intense the conflict. Boundaries are detrimental to spiritual growth for many reasons but most importantly they create violence. Where human beings are concerned, a boundary will always invite one side to take freedom from another.

Consider for a moment your internal response to just a few of these boundaries: Republican/Democrat, Christian/Muslim/Jew, heterosexual/homosexual, Catholic/Protestant. For most people the habitual response is to see these words as largely opposite and mostly irreconcilable positions. "Well, I am a (insert word here) and I know that X, Y, and Z are correct." This leads you to the unavoidable conclusion that your position on the issue is the right one and he, she, they are wrong.

This is not spirituality or freedom, and you are now half way down the road to suffering and violence. You have taken the first steps toward removing the freedom of another. This first step comes in the form of self-righteousness and then judgment. Then we act or don't act accordingly. All of the suffering we have inflicted on ourselves, each other, and everything else on earth is the result of what started as a word boundary.

I am not suggesting that all boundaries should be removed and everyone be allowed to behave as he or she sees fit. Spiritual freedom doesn't imply this. I am suggesting that if you are in pursuit of spiritual freedom you need to become aware of the boundaries you have constructed and the impact they have on who and what you are. Become aware of your boundaries and then ask yourself: do the boundaries in my life give me spiritual freedom? A boundary, even a word boundary (and they all start as word boundaries), is a place of conflict and stuckness, and this can never yield spiritual freedom.

The point is to always remember that words are not the truth; they only point toward the shadows of many truths. I believe this to be the case no matter who or what the source of the words may be, myself included. The point to remember is that spirituality is constructed out of your experience, it is not given to you by another. Fr. Frahm loved to tell the following story.

Satan was walking through the Garden of Eden with one of his friends. As they walked a little piece of the Truth fell from Satan's pocket and rolled down the path behind them and stopped at the foot of a tree. Just as Satan turned to go retrieve it, Adam ran out from the underbrush grabbed the small piece of the truth and ran away. Satan smiled and laughed. His friend looked at him and said, "Aren't you going to go take that back?" "No, said Satan, I'll let him write it down and make a doctrine of it, then I've got him."

Finally, I will talk a great deal about the divine and about God, but I do not know exactly what or who God is. Unlike much of the world around me I remain uncertain of God's identity, plan, desires, religious affiliation, and precise gender as well as how best to come into relationship with him or her. Many people and organizations apparently have this knowledge, as well as God's unlisted phone number, which they use to check their facts and receive classified directives. I don't have this either. I do not know who is correct or what orientation to God is best, but I know what Fr. Frahm would say. Do you really think it matters?

# Chapter One
# What's Your Distance From God?

The nature and limits of your spiritual freedom are reflected in the boundaries that exist between you and God. The fewer boundaries you have, the more freedom you have. The more freedom you have, the closer God is at this moment. Most of us, however, spend our time constructing and re-constructing new and improved boundaries designed to make us feel safe in the face of God's perceived absence or the world's perceived nastiness. All of our pain, guilt, shame, fear, anger, and loss are evidence that God is not present in ourselves, other people and the world. This sense of exile brings with it a deep sense of angst that compels us to set up boundaries to separate us and protect us from all that we do not accept, desire or approve of.

Here is an example of a common boundary. I opened my eyes this morning and I did not directly experience God; therefore she or he must be somewhere else. The "somewhere else" you have proposed is a boundary. It is a line you have drawn between you and God. This most fundamental of boundaries is fluid and ambiguous, and soon it will begin to generalize. Over time, every belief, cognition, and intuition will build upon it as a foundation. A boundary with this fundamental position will arrive at every moment just before you do and make it impossible to conceive of a world without it.

Fr. Frahm taught me about seeing and knowing this first and most primary boundary...the one between myself and God. I have come to agree with his assessment that all other boundaries - language, social, intra-psychic, interpersonal, or otherwise - are products of this first one. Your distance from God right now shapes everything.

Fr. Frahm taught me to acknowledge this boundary with honesty, touch it with compassion, and then to sit with it each and every day. He said the more I sit with it and see it for what it isn't, the easier it will be for me to cultivate the spiritual freedom necessary to let it go.

Spiritual freedom is the only human response to this first boundary, or any boundary, that allows us to move toward God. Fr. Frahm taught that spiritual freedom is a way of being, in which you can experience God right now, within your own heart and everywhere else, no matter what your past has been or what your future will be. All you need do to cultivate this freedom is earnestly begin to search for and sit with your boundaries.

Do not mistake this task for repetitious worship, faith-based dogma, or some temporary experience of ecstasy. These are common approaches to spiritual life but they are poor replacements for a basic, daily, human experience of the Divine. I am talking about being free to see and know God everywhere and in everything all the time. I'm not endorsing a charming notion in which you just believe the divine is present and then try to feel good about it. I'm not talking about the idea that God is in heaven but he's with me all the time. Ideas like this are thin and they make a poor soup that can't feed anyone for long.

The good news however, is that any boundary or separation between yourself and your God is actually an illusion and most likely one of your own creation. Therefore, you have two tasks. First, discover the illusion. Second, realize that no matter how real it seems, it doesn't matter.

If Fr. Frahm is correct, there is only the thinnest of curtains between God and you right this second. This curtain, thin as it is, keeps you from seeing and loving who you are and then loving God. Cultivating spiritual freedom will slowly dissolve this curtain and allow you to see everything, including yourself, for what it truly is...divine. As you can imagine, the experience of God everywhere may cause you to encounter the world in a different way.

I think it would be useful as well as appropriate if I offered an example of this freedom and how it impacts the way we see and understand the world. As you read, it is important to remember that I had been working with Fr. Frahm for many years prior to what I will describe, and now, years later, I still give up my freedom far more often than I would like. But, it's important to remember that the essence of spiritual freedom is the process, not the product.

It was a beautiful June day, and I had to make the three-hour drive to Lincoln for a meeting. I knew I would only be occupied for an hour and then I would have the rest of the day free. It seemed like such a waste to spend the day alone, so I called Fr. Frahm and asked if he wanted to ride along. The day was almost perfect, and a ride through the rolling hills of Eastern Nebraska promised to be unusually beautiful. He said he would love to go, and I picked him up at his home.

By this time in my life, Fr. Frahm was my best friend as well as my teacher, and I had known him for almost ten years. He had helped me let go of an anger and self-destruction that, given more time, would have consumed me. With this gift, he had become everything to me—a kind of best friend, father, and teacher all rolled into one.

After my appointment and lunch we were on our way home. He asked if I would turn before we came to Wahoo and drive past the home in which he had grown up. Unlike myself, Fr. Frahm had a painful childhood at the hands of his parents, both of whom abused him both physically and mentally. We turned onto the gravel and traveled a short distance north. He pointed and said, "There it is; we should stop here." We parked at the corner and he stared at the house. It was rather plain. The standard four up and four down square home that is common in the rural Midwest, grey faded paint with white trim and a few outbuildings around it, sitting on a hill with a small windbreak of trees on the north side. The current tenants were not farmers, so everything had a quiet, empty appearance.

For some time, I watched him look at that house. Soon the tears began to run down his cheeks. He had the look of someone remembering things and people now gone. He never made a sound, and although I wanted to speak, I thought it best not to intrude.

Finally, he turned to me and said, "That taught me pretty much what I thought it would." I had long since stopped letting his more cryptic remarks go by unquestioned. "What did you learn?" I asked. He stared out the window and said, "I used to think that what happened here destroyed my childhood, and God must have turned a blind eye to it all. Because of that, I was a prisoner of this place for half my life. The truth is that they were doing the best they knew how. As I have grown older I have come to understand that what I needed they couldn't give me. What I needed God couldn't give me. If you want to be free, the thing you need most you have to find inside yourself, and to find it you have to realize that it doesn't matter."

I sat in the sun and thought about what he had said. In my own life, I found this idea easier to understand than to practice. I wanted so much to be free of the anger and fear inside me. But at the end of the day I had never understood how these things could "not matter." My thinking spiraled into nothing and soon I could only stare at my feet. I looked up at him and he smiled at me. He reached out and put his hand on my cheek. He had a way of looking at me in which I could see whatever I needed reflected in his eyes. I looked, and I saw love.

He sat at that corner and looked directly into the most terrible things a human life can hold, and he wept. Yet here he was, looking at me, and all I could see was love. Everything became very still; even the wind slowed and became quiet. "It doesn't really matter," he said. "It hurts, yes, but it doesn't really matter at all."

For years, he had helped me sort out the fear I carried inside me. I had spent my life working to build a self that was not terrorized or nullified by the fact that my life would end. All I wanted was to be free of this fear. But I had encountered death twice in my youth, far sooner than I was equipped to deal with it. The first time it came I was a child and someone sitting right across the table from me got up walked into the next room and died. It returned when I was a teenager and it took my father. I learned quickly that death was something I should fear. I also learned I was helpless against it and there was no reason for it that made any sense to me at all. How could all of this not matter? Maybe it was the beautiful day, maybe it was the perfect moment, or maybe I had done everything I needed to do, but as I looked out the window, my whole world began to change.

It hit me. He did not want to stop here for himself. He went back and sat at the threshold of all that pain for me. He went back to that house so that I might find what I was looking for. He bathed in the anger, fear, and pain of his own childhood so that I could see how it was done and know it wouldn't kill me or at least wouldn't kill anything that mattered. He did it so I would know that I had to find what I was looking for inside me. All he could do was show me how.

He looked at me, and for some time didn't say anything. I sat for that moment inside the largest love I have ever known. I wanted an adult self that was not afraid of dying, that was not always angry. But as long as I held onto what I wanted I was stuck. I had to stop constructing the boundaries that had become the very thing from which I needed to free myself. The memories started to appear and I found myself looking at two decades of suffering. I breathed, Fr. Frahm smiled, and then it all faded away. In that moment, surrounded by love, I looked into the eyes of what terrified me, and it ceased to matter. Everything I thought I was, every boundary I had, disappeared and love was all that remained.

I'm not able to adequately describe this moment to you. It was not a feeling or a mere change of attitude. It was the most mundane, completely normal, and at the same time absolutely extraordinary, thing that has ever happened to me. Whatever boundaries I had disintegrated, and everything began to change. It was all very different, but also remained the same. In that moment there were no boundaries between myself and the world around me. I had become part of the immense loving everything that surrounded me. I also realized that this love had always existed and always would. In that moment, "I" did not exist. "I" was absorbed by something much larger.

It was the end of a mystery that had taken me some thirty odd years to stumble into. I looked over at Fr. Frahm. He was smiling. I felt my first sense of freedom, but it was a different kind of freedom. The fear and anger were still there. They just didn't matter as much. They had become transparent, and behind them all that remained was love. Nothing about me that had been real a moment ago was real any more. I was free for the first time in my life because "I" did not matter. In that moment, there was freedom. Not because I had put something behind me but because there was no "me" to put anything behind. I was gone and God was all that was left. This was not the freedom I had searched for nor was it the freedom I expected. This was another kind of freedom.

# Chapter Two
# Another Kind of Freedom

Take a moment to consider the notion that freedom is not a specific thing, idea, or concept. I think it is most true to say that freedom just is. Right now, at this moment, you are completely free to exist, or not, in any manner you wish. In truth, you and I have more freedom than we are capable of understanding. Ask yourself, "Am I free?" Or, as you read on, are the boundaries of your freedom coming into your awareness?

Freedom is life with no man-made boundaries. It is the natural shape of all levels of existence until a human mind shows up and imposes a boundary of some sort. Our most common boundaries come into existence when we relate to life by attempting to possess and manage it. With these boundaries our freedom shrinks dramatically. We take only small pieces of freedom, redesign them to meet our desires and address our fears, and then suggest that this is all there is. This truncated, redesigned freedom becomes the only way we can see, think, and feel. Then, it becomes our world.

As a result of our need to truncate freedom, natural freedom doesn't get a lot of attention because it does not serve our needs, individually or collectively. It is of no use, which is another way of saying that no individual, group, country, etc., can use it for anything. We cannot box it up and use it to make our lives better without the whole concept becoming meaningless, or worse, hypocritical. But the fact remains that our tendency as human beings is to do exactly that. We minimize real freedom and work to redesign it into something we can possess... and use.

Contemporary American culture has become quite expert at constructing definitions of freedom that are extraordinarily small and useful. Any connection our culture may have to a real, natural freedom is slowly fading in today's blinding light of patriotism, fundamentalism, conservatism, liberalism, and other "isms." Be it religion, politics, government, public policy, social cause or health care, organized entities of one form or another are spending extensive amounts of time and money to minimize and control what freedom is and therefore what freedom does.

Our favorite method of minimizing freedom has been to define it as democracy, or liberty, and then to slowly materialize it into something that can be possessed, bought, sold, loaned, or given away. This brand of freedom is something we can display to others as correct, and firmly in our possession. We are therefore entitled to use it as the rationale for controlling and punishing those whom we don't like or agree with, all the while suggesting that you don't ask any questions or look any further because this is the only correct perception.

This phenomenon has evolved to the point of ridiculousness. All people from the President to the local car dealer wrap themselves in the symbols of freedom to suggest that they are on the side of right and good. "And, by the way, please agree with my positions and please buy my cars. See how committed to freedom I am! How could I not be right and how could you not buy my product, agree with my position, or use my service?" We have spun and blurred freedom to such an extent that it no longer reflects anything but the shallow, materialistic cause that happens to be using it that day.

Above and beyond all of the propaganda from all of the usual suspects, freedom is the business of the human heart and the human soul. Freedom is the primary source of your growth and development as a human being. Freedom and the process of freedom are the only elements of this life that enlarge our humanity and bring use closer to God. Other avenues are available, but none of them will set you free.

What is your freedom like? Ask yourself what freedom means to you. Initially, you will probably get the educational and media conditioning that you have been fed throughout your life. I encourage you to take a moment and go beyond this as much as you can.

*What must happen and what must you have in order to be free?*

*What must the other person do or have in order for you to be free?*

The goal of questions like this is to acquaint you with the notion that most of your conceptions and practices of freedom are self-serving. They work to make you feel safe and secure in your day-to-day functioning. They serve to make you feel good about who you are and what you think and feel. Most of us, until we begin to think about it, know no other way to come into relationship with freedom except to use it.

If we are honest with ourselves, our freedom is a construction that serves our desires and needs. It serves us individually, culturally, religiously, and politically. It is an extension of our personal narcissism and ultimately our collective narcissism. This narcissism can be defined as: "My freedom is right, just, and correct, and your conception and practice of freedom, if it does not agree with mine, is wrong." No matter what or who the source of this argument may be, its logical extension is this: "I am correct and entitled to my freedom and you, if you disagree with me, are wrong, dishonest, misleading, and/or bad. I am thereby justified in doing whatever I need to do to you."

We don't have to look far to find confirmation that narcissistic, self-serving freedom is our culture's chosen perspective. It is our primary everyday mode of interaction. We live in a place in which everyone is led to believe that nothing should impinge in any way on the needs of the individual and by extension his or her group.

Stare blankly at any form of media you wish. You will be bombarded with the idea that you should be able to do anything and own anything. You should never be sick, feel down, or experience discomfort. People who choose to cause you discomfort—physical, mental or spiritual—should be sanctioned or criminalized. No matter where you look or what you listen to, the message is coming... over and over. It is coming because we want it. We have embraced it. We live by it. It makes us feel safe and righteous.

Whatever you choose to call it, or however you chose to justify it, this is not freedom. True freedom exists in and of itself. It exists independent of you. The smaller freedom, the freedom most of us embrace, originates in the human mind.

At the level of your psychology and biology, whatever is in your best interests is best. Whatever propagates your happiness, and by extension, your survival, is good and correct. Outside, above, and behind all the attractive political, social, psychological, and moral posturing is and will always be the best interests of the individual mind and its operator, the ego-self.

Why is the ego-self so important? How could it possibly lie at the bottom of an issue like freedom? The answer is simple. The ego-self looks at the human life and it is terrified. Deep inside you, the ego-self knows that you are finite, and not only finite but unpredictably so. This idea is terrifying to a structure that is completely and solely invested in its own survival.

Sit back in your chair, take a breath, and relax. When you are comfortable, say out loud to yourself, "I am going to die and I have no idea when." Try not to do, say, or think anything and see what comes into your awareness. Is your first experience one in which you reason it away? "I'm going to live for a long time yet. I'm only 38." Do you become anxious or concerned? "You know, my mom had cancer; they say it's genetic." Are you unable to cope with the idea at all and just shut down or forget the whole thing? "I'm not going to worry about this; it's ridiculous."

Your response to the exercise should tell you something about what your ego-self is doing. How do you (your mind/ego-self) deal with this issue? Most of us would rather not go there. This is a normal response. The reality, however, is that almost everything we do in our lives is directly and/or indirectly, consciously and/or unconsciously, an attempt to deny or overcome the fate that we know awaits us.

Each person, due to the particular needs, wants, and desires of his or her ego-self, approaches the problem differently. Each of us will choose a path that helps deny, control, or otherwise manage our oncoming, ultimate fate. Some turn to possessions, using "things" to distract them from what is waiting at the end. Others turn to activities such as business, work, politics, or a specific cause. They feel that if they achieve, accomplish, and/or overcome enough they will never have to address what is approaching from behind.

Still others and this is the most common approach, turn to a religion, and adopt a set of beliefs that will protect them from the notion that death renders everything meaningless. Everything in life from hobbies and fantasies to spirituality and character is built by an ego-self that works vigorously, 24-7, to stay one step ahead of its own undoing.

To let you off the hook to some extent, much of this process is biological. It is the voice of a genome that only knows it is good to live on and multiply. The drive to be happy, fulfilled, and survive is a voice that lives in every cell of your body. It is alive inside you and it might be more true to say it is your life. Psychologically it is the same. Neurons fire at the whim of this same genome, and at a cognitive level, its voice rings out both consciously and unconsciously every moment of every day. You should eat, drink, and be happy and you should not die. Every gene, every cell, every organ, every process, and every thought is driven by an energy that only knows it is better to be alive than not.

To see the cosmos as it truly is, brutal, chaotic, indifferent, circular, and yet all the while divine, is devastating to the ego-self because it makes the construction of a secure, confident, everyday existence impossible. The curse, the original sin, of the human ego-self is that it is doomed from the day it is born to try and escape its own finite situation. And very quickly, the human mind must marshal a consistent and comprehensive ego-self structure or it will be overcome and begin to break down. This repetitive and compulsive process is the rock we must roll up hill only to see it roll back to the bottom, where we must start the ascent again or suffer greatly.

I am not saying that the ego-self serves no useful purpose in the development of the human being. It is the primary integrating system of the mind/brain. Its existence allows the developing human to construct the resources necessary for an unstable and fragmented self to live in the world.

In the big picture of modern culture however, the strong confident ego-self has become the only desired end. The security-hungry and self-serving ego has become the stopping place. We see nothing beyond it. Therefore we consider nothing else possible or even necessary. This compulsion to construct security produces constant insecurity. This insecurity drives the process that turns freedom into a small, self-interested tool that we use to create an illusion.

The only way a human being can succeed in the attempt to construct an independent, self-sufficient ego-self that does not have to address its impending demise is to build, participate in, and exist inside an illusion. A person must project his or her ego-self and its contents—will, belief, desire and fantasy—onto the world in order to manufacture a new and kinder truth. This ego-self must coerce, control, deny, destroy, or join everything within the world that is threatening in an effort to construct the security needed to escape a constant state of anxiety.

The result is a fantasy, an illusion in which the world is no longer self-contradictory, interconnected, deceptive, paradoxical, indifferent, and dangerous, yet all the while divine at its core. We deny the real world and like real freedom, we no longer see it. The world we agree on, the only one we will accept or acknowledge is one that doesn't change or is at least controllable and understandable. We work to design a world in which no one suffers and there is one (or very few) correct and divinely acknowledged right ways to do and see everything.

We expand this infantile illusion about the way the world ought to be or the way we wish it was and apply it to everything including our God in a effort to promote security in a world we do not understand or at least does not understand us. It is narcissism at its most effective. It is the ego-self at its zenith.

The need for this illusion is compulsive in all human beings. Your ego-self and the mind it lives in is, to you, the epicenter of the universe. Under normal circumstances it is the only place in which you can feel yourself exist. It is imperative psychologically, biologically, and genetically to preserve this existential homestead.

This commandment of existence is strong fuel for an illusion. With a compulsive ego-self in control, the ideas that best serve the individual and his/her social, political, business, entertainment, health, religious, and moral needs become seductive. Over a very short period of time a seduction will become an ideology. These ideologies participate in the denial and repression necessary to almost stabilize a fragile human existence in the face of what is real: paradox, chaos, death, and, oh yes, lower taxes.

I said "almost" because the constant confrontation with impending non-existence never really goes away. It only steps back for a moment to wait until the next opportunity to present itself. No matter how much you grasp at ideology, dogma, possessions, notoriety, money or other attempts at truncated freedom, the threat will never completely disappear. It only fades away and returns with stronger evidence that you are more impermanent than ever.

The result of this scenario is a hole inside you, a sense that you are missing something significant, something that would make you, your life, and your world secure and fulfilling. Whether you experience this sense of lack as anxiety about the future, regret about the past, or desire in the present moment, it makes no difference. These things are different forms of the same problem. No matter what you have done to address them they probably changed very little. If you are trying to build an illusion, success is and can only be temporary. This constant encounter with anxiety creates a longing for something more. The problem is that inside an illusion, with only minimal freedom, this longing can never be filled.

You cannot successfully free yourself of this longing because the underlying assumptions you hold about it are flawed. Because you do not understand, you could use up your entire life struggling with an illusion. The more you fight to be free the more you experience suffering and do violence to yourself and others. Suffering and violence lead only to more and stronger longing. The problem is circular. It cannot solve itself.

In your attempts to satisfy the longing, your ego-self works relentlessly to free itself of the anxiety that constantly whispers that you are not adequate enough to construct a secure existence. The voice of your ego-self sounds like this: *You are God's special little (insert name here,) and he loves you very much. You live in the greatest country in the world, a country sanctioned by God. Your beliefs, ethics, morals, and actions are correct and best for you, your group, and everyone around you and your group. You should not suffer, be unhappy, or have anything unjustly put upon you. You deserve to have what you desire.*

There are two problems here that deserve mention since they are weapons that are directly responsible for much of the suffering in our world. First, you can repeat the above paragraph to yourself as many times as you like, in as many ways as you like, and nothing will really change. You will still long to find something to take the place of what you lack. You will still have to search for something that will make your existence infinite in some fashion. Create a better illusion made of more effective medical care or a more intense illusion with bigger and louder entertainment and still nothing changes.

We can sum the second problem up as follows: Everyone can't have this type of self-serving freedom at the same time. This rule is also applicable to every group, society, culture, country, government, and religious institution. If my freedom looks different than yours, (and it will) and I must have it, our only choice is conflict. Much of the suffering inside you and in the world around you directly results from the fact that everyone possesses this same sense of freedom regarding themselves and their country, business, religion, ethics, and actions. The freedom we work so hard to manufacture will almost always bring us into conflict.

The only thing that can address the longing of the human being is spiritual freedom. This freedom exists before human beings, not as a product of attempts to control insecurity. It is the natural state of the universe and it has no interest or investment in your ego-self. The paradox here is that the more you attempt to strengthen the ego-self the more you distance yourself from spiritual freedom. To find release from your ego-self is to let go of the boundaries that stand between you and the divine. This ego-self, this "I" you think you are, has to wither and ultimately dissolve for whatever is behind it to be free.

So how do we begin to develop spiritual freedom? What is it that makes this freedom so powerful that it can move us beyond the ego-self? The answer to both these questions is love. Love is the only path to freedom. It is the only force that can release a human being from itself.

# Chapter Three
# The Foundation of Love

The love that cultivates spiritual freedom is not the romantic, sentimental, or erotic love that we see everywhere around us. Nevertheless, everything in our culture, from education to media, suggests that romance, sentiment, and eros are the paths we should choose in order to be happy. Each one of these however, is sustained by the ego-self and suggests that we should engage in love to make us feel happy, secure or fulfilled. As a result of living this way, we come to embody the idea that love is about "me" or "I," and we struggle to acquire the abilities necessary for an authentic, honest connection with whomever and whatever we love.

The stark reality is that if you meet the world as an "I," then your love will very often be unfulfilling, frustrating and difficult to sustain. The evidence that we struggle to love anything beyond ourselves is not hard to find. Divorce rates, interpersonal violence, geo-political violence, bigotry, racism, and intolerance are rampant. We covet what we desire, possess it, try to control it, and call this love. What we cannot control, or relate to, we frequently reject completely. And we don't just reject it, we label it as bad or wrong.

This kind of love will never move anyone beyond the boundaries that contain them. It does exactly the opposite. Everything relates to the "I." What is good for me is good. What is not good for me is bad. Although this state of affairs is understandable and even predictable, it cannot move you toward spiritual freedom. This kind of love is the product of the ego-self and it tends to generate more boundaries than it transcends. It becomes an extension of our personal narcissism, albeit a socially acceptable one.

Without deliberate time and effort, few people are even aware that they can love in a different way. So we sit in the middle of what we have created and complain that something is wrong. I think the answer to the question of what is wrong can be best summed up as follows: Love is either everywhere, in everything and for everyone or it is not really love. You either work to love everything and everyone or your love of others is actually about you. You are doing what is best and easiest for you.

Love is not a mysterious external force that lands on the lucky ones and abandons others. It is not given by God as a gift or removed from you for bad behavior. Those who suggest that God hands out love to those who obey him are only pushing their own agenda, and dragging God down to their level. Love that is capable of nurturing spiritual freedom is not something that happens or doesn't happen to you. It is not a thing to be possessed or rejected, found or lost. Plainly put, this type of love is not external in any way. It is not outside of you at all.

Love that can transcend boundaries and cultivate freedom is a particular way of being alive. It is built on the foundation of authentic, honest action. As many people have said before, love is a verb. It is what you do. A love that can cultivate spiritual freedom is something you do everyday authentically and honestly. To whatever degree you're able, today, you put yourself aside and act toward others and the world with love.

This is not terribly complicated and there is no pressure to get it spot-on correct. As with all elements of spiritual life it only matters that you do it. It is not how you love or who you love that matters. All that matters is that you love. You authentically and honestly come from wherever you are and choose to love in whatever manner you can. It is the choice to love, without judgment, that moves you toward freedom.

Your choice cannot be strategic or manipulative. It cannot be done in order to gain something or somehow improve your situation. It is also important to note that it is very difficult to love with judgment. You cannot really love the person but dislike or disapprove of who or what they are. This is a semantic two-step that is all two frequent in today's world. Put simply, you cannot love part of someone without damaging the other person and also yourself.

When you choose to love without boundaries you are not compelled to see your world through the eyes of your ego. The practice of loving without bound-aries develops your ability to be honestly aware of other people and available for relationship with them. This situation is in direct opposition to the strategic or judgmental approaches to love which leave you in relationship with what you think the other person is or what you want them to be.

A daily practice of love will help you start to remove the boundaries between you and other people, the world and God. When the boundaries go, your illusions go with them. As your "I" fades away what remains is graceful open space with no investment in "this" or "that". In this place all there is, is love. All there is, is God Here you will find freedom, spiritual freedom. You see, love can really change your world.

It is the daily process of loving that is the key to this life. It is very difficult, if not impossible, to understand your own being, find meaning in this existence or experience God if you cannot or will not love. You need the act of love and the spiritual freedom that it cultivates to engage in a creative, rebellious and transformative human life. The treasures of this existence are not given to you because you exist or because you ask. These are excuses people use to avoid their responsibility of their lives. To find spiritual freedom, you have to cultivate it in the blood, sweat, tears, joys and bliss of this moment.

For most of us, spiritual freedom can only bloom in the imperfect soil of a loving relationship with another being. Neither isolated self-interest nor shallow interaction is sufficient to provide the elements necessary for freedom to fully develop. The love that emerges out of a relationship between two beings who work to care for one another brings creative transformation to both people involved. When you come from a place of love, you are much more likely to see the other person, and the world, for what they are, rather than what you believe them, or want them, to be. More importantly, when you see things a little more clearly, particularly your boundaries, you will find it easier to love yourself. This is the first step to loving other people and then loving God.

The essence of your life is revealed in your ability to love. Now take a few moments and sit with the following questions.

*Can you love other people, no matter what?*
*Can you feel love when it is offered to you?*
*Will you risk for it?*
*Can you accept love when it is offered to you?*

These questions will tell you a lot about your boundaries. Ask yourself these questions again, and be honest. These explorations do you little good if you can't take the time to really asses your response. If your understanding and practice of love never expands beyond the initial and the superficial, then you are cheating yourself. Only by authentically and honestly pursuing your truth will your love transcend itself and move toward freedom.

So how can you love differently? Where does it come from? How can you and I nurture it? The answer is learning; you learn to love. You actively choose to love everyday. You engage in relationship(s), and in the process, you'll learn. Simple, old-fashioned trial and error learning is the key. You have to just get out there and choose to do it, but you will probably have to do things differently than you have done them in the past.

If you are looking for spiritual freedom, love is the starting point and mistakes are the outcome you want. Few of us learn from our successes, and fewer yet learn anything significant. Begin to develop a practice of love and then get out there and love others. No one else can explain to you how you should do this. I can offer you some guidelines and point to what I consider to be important, but that's all. You have to begin the journey not knowing exactly what you are doing.

Like all spiritual issues, love has no correct method. (And beware those who claim to possess the correct method.) There is only what you choose to do. Be aware of what you're doing, enter relationship, and love from this place. With enough practice your love will give you glimpses of the world beyond your ego-self, but pay attention here because this next point is important. You learn to love yourself first, then you can love others, and then you can love God. It has to happen in this order because if you can't do the first it will be impossible to do the second or the third. With effort (and a bit of luck) you will one day find yourself standing in the middle of what you want. Love is sneaky that way. By the time you notice it, you're in it up to your waist.

# Chapter Four
# Witnessing a Life

Fr. Frahm said repeatedly that what is real in the human being lives below and behind the more acceptable characteristics that we call "self." But because this thing we are is not pretty and in many cases not accepted by others, we cannot possibly be this person. So we construct a different face for the world and pretend that this is what we really are. Our difficulty accepting who and what we are makes it almost certain that we will not be able to understand or tolerate our deeper and more human reality. This moves us toward a life of consistently superficial and shallow daily experience. Fr. Frahm taught that if you were going to go looking for what and who you really are, and you were serious about it, you would need to have a witness.

Cognitions, thoughts, memories, and mental constructions are not real in a human sense. They are the habitual internal constructions of a self that is, to a large extent, mired in an illusion. To be real, Fr. Frahm said your experience must emerge from what is true inside you and exist between you and at least one other human being. Having another person witness the truth of your life requires you to take responsibility for your experience and choose with deliberate intent to own it or reject it. In the space between you and another person you are less able to hide behind illusion, semantics, fuzzy logic or just utter bull. This clarity gives you the opportunity to see things for what they are and not what you thought they were or wanted them to be. More importantly, another person can acknowledge your experience as real and you can witness their response to you. This further adds to the actual human reality of what is happening. In this exchange it becomes possible to accept and hold the deeper and more honest elements of what you are. This, according to Fr. Frahm, is how people change and grow.

Human beings need to take responsibility for their lives. They need to come to terms with whom and what they actually are, with what they really think and feel. Having our lives witnessed and acknowledged by at least one other person is one way to do this. To witness the life of another you need only listen with compassion and know how to keep your mouth shut. Having your experience witnessed, according to Fr. Frahm, is how you discover the authentic and honest being within you. Then it is possible to escape the narrow confines of our everyday illusion and allow your daily experience to be a stepping stone to creativity, revelation and authentic living. Without a process of witnessing you are left isolated and disconnected from the life and world around you.

The idea of having our lives witnessed by another is quite peculiar. Most of us will immediately start to think of either religious confession or the psychotherapeutic endeavor. But this is not a religious undertaking and it definitely lacks the artificially constructed framework and rules of therapy. All of the talk about forgiveness, superiority, inferiority, defense mechanisms, introverts, extroverts, character, personality, and lifestyle applies only to the self we create. These ideas have little contact with what is real inside us. Religion, psychology, counseling, and the self-help gurus have always been either stubbornly ignorant of this fact or ridiculously dishonest about what they can really do for another person. If either of them could deliver as promised we would have a lot less suffering in this world.

There is a more radical and true being that lurks beneath the layers you call (insert your name here). This being is the core toward which everything human and spiritual gravitates. All other dimensions of self, such as personality or character, are creations of the mind or ego-self. They are the outermost skin on a very large onion.

I would venture a guess that on some deeper level many of us know this. We know that when we lie in bed, alone in the dark, the thing that emerges is not the self we show to the public or at times even to other parts of ourselves. This thing, this being, is primitively solid and for the most part immune to change, therapeutic or otherwise. It is completely alive and ever present, with a nature, logic and perception all its own. Our real being is, for the most part, private and will never offer itself up to be witnessed by the everyday world. Some aspects of who we are belongs only to us, and must remain ours alone.

In its simplest form the only thing that is real inside you is consciousness. The more radical and true being that I've been speaking about is the unique shape taken by the consciousness within you. For each of us, consciousness is different. Our basic structure may be the same but it is our will, experience, environment and biology that give shape what we are. More importantly however, your individual consciousness is but a small part of a much larger consciousness that permeates and holds everything in the cosmos. If you are a human being, it is Being. If you are a person this larger consciousness is God.

Your consciousness however, is largely at the mercy of an ego-self that wants to be unique, special, safe and independent. Your ego-self does not want to be defined as a small, non-unique, non-special part of something much larger and it certainly doesn't want to be defined as non-real. So, the ego-self goes about the business of making sure it is the only reality. You've heard it at work. It says that you are unique and separate from every other person or thing. It says you are alone and a part of nothing else.

The result of this ongoing process is a boundary(s) that exiles your true being from its source, the larger consciousness or God. But each day of your life, the consciousness beneath and behind your ego-self longs for what it lost. It longs to reconnect with the larger consciousness. It longs to reconnect with God. I have come to believe, with Fr. Frahm's help, that it is this longing that drives the human life.

With all this in mind, I think it's only fair if I lead by example. Therefore, the rest of this section is a very brief account of my life and my relationship to Fr. Frahm. I have put this on paper because I too need someone to witness my life in order for it to change and become something else. It just so happens that I have chosen you, or more accurately we have chosen each other. I hope that we can do this well, and we both will have an opportunity to grow.

I have known many people who were born open to relationship and drawn to connection with others. I also know people like myself who were born with the strong intuition that they are alone. Some children realize quite early that they have been thrown into a world in which they are not really connected to anything or anyone. Or at least not connected in the way people around them seem to be. This knowledge causes problems for them as they grow older because they can never escape it for more than a moment. It stands over their shoulder no matter what they do. This is not a psychological problem or behavioral deficit. It is simply the reality of that particular human being.

As children these individuals are almost always ill-equipped to fool themselves about their situation. They cannot manufacture a fulfilling sense of connection to others no matter how hard they try. They are not amenable to therapy, instruction or learning in this matter. They are alone and they know it. If they are unable to face this directly, the only option they have to live otherwise is to pretend.

I was born alone into a loving family of other people who I suspect are also alone. I think it's quite likely that alone people have alone children, although I hold out for the possibility that at least some people learn to be alone. I wish I could say that I learned to be this way, but that's not true. I have always been alone. Wherever our souls come from before birth, they come with strong inclinations, emotions, and orientations already in their nature. Our slates are most certainly not blank, and more importantly they come with cracks, chips, and other characteristics that can set the trajectory for an entire life. I have a suspicion that we arrive here already largely who we are. As far as being born to other alone people, well, maybe we are attracted to like souls. The reason is unimportant, but my slate was shaped in a way that affected everything that was to be written on it.

Being alone is difficult but it's not the end of the world. Solitude will make you vulnerable in your own particular way, but I survived just as everyone else does. My early life was a beautiful one made up of daily explorations into the hills, groves, ponds, creeks, and farm buildings of rural western Iowa. I developed a propensity to disappear during these excursions for long periods of time. This habit, in which I initially pretended to be my father, and then other people, tested my imagination as well as my mother's blood pressure.

My father had, through no fault of his own, lost his chance to have his own farm. As a result, he worked as a hired man for other people. Nothing draws a child like working with the earth, and he was the earth to me. I wanted to be with him and to be him. I followed him down the hill and pretended that I was working with him. I also did this at home or the neighbor's place. My imagination was sufficiently vivid that in this process I often got distracted, tired or both.

Because of this, my playing farmer had several inherent dangers. First, I often turned the equipment on and forgot to turn it off. This exhausted the battery, and it didn't take long to figure out who the culprit was. One or two instances of this are enough to build quite a reputation. With little in the way of direct supervision, I caused so many problems that I was forced to blame my actions on the neighbor's dog. Unfortunately for me, Jack had an honest face and when they confronted him he always looked completely innocent. And he had no opposable thumb. Justice was often swift.

I was also prone to taking a nap wherever I happened to be playing at the time. This left my mother unable to find me. In those instances when my nap took up most of the afternoon, my mother would begin searching for me and calling the neighbors to see if I was there. Her search on at least one occasion became an actual dragnet in which the neighbors had to stop their work and comb the fields, just in case I had decided to lie down in the alfalfa and go to sleep. When they eventually found me, my mother was an interesting combination of thankful and angry. But leaning more toward angry.

The current obsession with the safety of children did not exist in the early 1970's. My childhood was a wonderful time filled with lawn darts and completely devoid of bicycle helmets and knee pads. Given today's propaganda, I should be able to look back at my many friends with traumatic head injuries and facial disfigurations and regret our stupidity and lack of safety equipment. But we all made it, and that leaves me to suspect that today's safety obsession may be less about children and more about other things.

The upshot of all this is that I was free. There is no replacement for a childhood filled with this kind of freedom. The imagination flourishes and becomes almost too bold to be contained. The conjunction of an authentic life and individual imagination is the epicenter of creativity. In this place, we create our life each day rather than living it. It is here that our real personhood develops. Your and I are real and alive to the extent that each day finds us thinking and saying things we didn't know we knew. This is growth. This is learning. The rest is just education.

If you have a unique vulnerability, life has a way of pointing it out for you. I didn't realize it at the time, but I first saw mine at the age of four when I stood at the graveside of my great-grandmother. She was a beautiful, almost ancient Cherokee woman who always seemed kind of magical to me. I had only seen her a handful of times and then suddenly she was gone.

She was much darker than I was (my father was adopted) and had a deeply lined face with white hair. I was always struck by how different she was from everything and everyone around her. She liked to ask questions that required me to imagine something, like where I would live when I grew up. She would think deeply about my answer and either agree or offer some new direction. One time she looked at me and told me what I would look like when I grew older. I believed her completely. And for the most part, she was right.

She was magical because she loved her life, and she seemed to love everyone else, including me. Though I saw her only a few times as a child, she always took the time to speak with me instead of at me, but most importantly, she possessed the ability to hear. This ability is far rarer than people think. Most people work very hard to only hear what they want to hear. If you are an alone child, it is amazing when you run into someone who can actually hear you and then treats what you say with importance. It seems that grandparents more than any other group of people offer this blessing to children.

I remember it as a cold day but my mother tells me this isn't true. I guess that my memory, like all memory, has land for sale. I also remember being caught up in my own discomfort and being agitated. When I looked up, some man was pouring my great-grandmother's ashes on the ground. I watched him as he emptied the box and then shook it to get the stragglers. I knew what a funeral was and what a graveyard was, and I came to this event with the expectation that my Grandmother was going to "be" somewhere. I became terrified when I saw what was left of her begin to blow away.

It never ceases to amaze me that the sum total of a human life can be transported to its final address in a six by nine inch cardboard box. But, I have seen it happen on three occasions now. Six by nine seems too small to hold a person's life, and cardboard does no justice to someone you knew and loved. I still recall watching the grey and white ashes that were once my Grandmother float off across the frozen ground in a stiff breeze. I began to panic, and I cried loudly to my parents that she was blowing away. I'm sure they said something to comfort me, but I don't recall now what it was. I do remember that every time I looked back, more of her was gone.

This event confirmed for an alone child that not only was I alone, but there was a nothingness called death that was out there waiting for me. And apparently, there was no way to stave it off. The most loving and magical person I had ever known had been reduced to ashes and then just blew away in a bitterly cold morning wind. If this was the ending of someone as wonderful as she, then I had reason to be concerned.

I have always been prone to analyze my life, even as a young child. I considered this event almost daily for some time. My pondering did little to help me. In fact, it brought only more uncertainty and fear. I was lost and I began to seriously crave attention from, and connection with, other people to feel safe. Connected to another person, I gained a false sense of security that would, for a short time, make me forget that I was afraid.

In order to get what I needed I acted for other people. I acted like the person I thought they wanted me to be. Usually I acted like the person I wanted attention from. This process was complicated by the fact that I wasn't all that likable when I wanted attention, which soon became all the time. I tended, like most beginning actors, to go too far too fast. As my need for safety became larger, I was forced to do my over-the-top performance for security full time. I acted everywhere and always. I acted so well that at some point I forgot I was acting.

I tried the normal things to help me belong as a child, but none were terribly effective. I went to school and played with friends. We rode our bikes and went into the dark wet places that only children go. I did it all exactly like I should have. Most of the time, however, I felt like I was on the other side of a glass window. I could see it, hear it, and do it with them, but I always felt separate. I could never understand why I was so anxious when I was doing what everyone else was doing. The more separate I felt, the more I acted to get attention, and with it the security that comes from connection. This pattern filled most of my childhood with desperation and wild exaggerations.

As I grew older, I learned to control my longing for connection and security with an interesting combination of denial and self-sufficiency. I pretended that either I didn't feel afraid or I was too strong to worry about it. Neither of these methods did anything but mask what was becoming a very real problem for me. As time went on, my attempts to find and connect with others became more anxiety provoking. If the other person was unavailable, or would back away from me by even an inch, I would become anxious and then angry. No matter what I did or how many people I was in relationship with, the feeling of fear never went away. The more afraid I was, the more anxious and angry I became. Then my behavior would become, let's say, colorful.

One day it happened. I was talking to some classmates and trying to be funny. If you're going to act you need to go with your strengths, and apparently I have the right genes for funny. We were laughing and enjoying our recess when suddenly I realized that I was acting for them. Not acting funny, but acting like "myself." I was acting this way because I didn't know what else to do or be. I had acted so long I had lost contact with anything else inside myself. I became confused, ended the conversation quickly, and walked away. Although I didn't really understand this incident, it bothered me for some time. I started to think that something was wrong with me, and I know now that I was beginning to suspect the real problem. I was unable to connect with other people because I was unable to find myself.

It wasn't always this way. No matter how uncomfortable or even impossible I made my world, I could always find comfort in the outdoors. It drew me in and filled my world with creeks, ponds, and acres of country filled with wild things. Everywhere were trails made by cattle and other animals just waiting to be explored. Old abandoned building filled with memories and time invited me in. In the natural world I found places that seemed to be as alone as I felt. I began to wonder if nature held some type of secret about being alone and if I looked hard enough I would find it.

Being outdoors almost every day saved my childhood from the aloneness that surrounded it. Somewhere between the sight of fireflies and the scent of fresh mown hay I felt connected to something. I could sink into the seasonal rhythms of the earth and let them hold me. I couldn't be alone because I was part of something else, something larger. The natural world was alive and was always willing to embrace me if I would slow down enough and become involved. As a child, I ran through trails lined with thistles to sit in quiet places and listen to the water. In these moments I glimpsed something that would take me another twenty years to find again. Out in the pasture, my aloneness didn't matter.

There was a little voice in my head, however, that never let me have peace for too long before it whispered again that something was missing. It whispered so much and so often that I began to accept that what it said was true, and maybe I was just kidding myself. Then one warm summer day, the first of two events occurred that took my suspicion of isolation and turned it into what it would be for many years to follow–fear.

The notion of who is a neighbor was an interesting concept in the Iowa of my youth. Neighbors were those joined by proximity who choose to take an interest in the well being of those around them. You didn't have to take an interest. Some didn't. But those who worked together could bring the hay in faster than those who worked alone. If you helped others, they helped you. Those who participated in each others' lives were neighbors.

Arlo was a neighbor. He was tall and his skin was darkened by the sun. Every time I saw him he wore the same hat and a serious five o'clock shadow. He was different because he wore his hat tipped slightly off to one side. In small town Iowa, how you wear your hat is as valid a personality test as the Rorschach–almost always an honest advertisement of what you can expect of the person underneath it. A hat worn slightly off to the side displays an ease of character and genuine openness.

Arlo had funny teeth, and he smiled and laughed a lot. He lured you with a story or joke into a situation in which you could laugh with him and at him at the same time. There were other Arlos in my youth, Noel, Al, Harold, Delbert,

Les, and Einer, to name just a few, but Arlo was the most Arlo'ish of them all. And his status with me was drastically elevated because he had a beautiful blond 1970's movie poster daughter. She wasn't my first love, but just about.

He lived some five miles east and had come to help Noel and Rodney put their hay into the barn. Hay was big job because of its sheer quantity and that it all has to be stored on the second floor of the barn. The more help you have with a project like this the better it is. The day was warm, and we had been working hard when afternoon lunch time came and everyone walked into the cool of the house. The deep rattle and hum of the air conditioner was welcoming, and it was accompanied by iced tea, coffee, dried beef sandwiches, and cake. Everyone sat around the table talking and enjoying the chance to rest.

Once we were inside the laughter started. Joking and teasing were skills that everyone around me seemed to possess and they were willing to sharpen them on each other given the opportunity. You had to develop a quick wit and a thick skin in order to keep up. You could tease occasionally when you worked but you had to stay focused, particularly on the equipment which could be dangerous. Lunch, on the other hand, was the time when you could ambush a lame member of the herd. Someone would say something stupid or simply look at someone else wrong and the production was off and running. Like sharks attracted to blood in the water, the poor soul would have all his less than perfect qualities pointed out and not so gentle advice was given regarding how the world might actually be better off without him in it. This ritual was merciless, and great respect was given to the person who could crush the other guy's self-esteem in such a way that he was reduced to confused mumbling.

That day, a cup of coffee, a sandwich, and many jokes later, Arlo got up and went into the other room and I got up and went outside to grab something. When I came back in the kitchen was empty. I looked into the living room and saw Arlo lying on the cold linoleum floor. Noel was doing CPR, someone was calling for the ambulance, and everyone else stood frozen. I walked into the room and stood there looking down at him. I knew he was dead and I got the distinct sense that everyone else knew it as well but they were doing what needed to be done. The CPR continued, and the ambulance came to take him away. As I watched it leave, I noticed that they never even turned on the lights. I didn't take it as a good sign.

I walked around that evening in a haze. I wanted to scream or cry or both, but I couldn't really do anything. It was like I couldn't feel my mouth well enough to scream out of it. Since I couldn't do anything I went about my business as if nothing had happened. What the hell, that's what everyone else was doing. The rest of that evening was very quiet.

Looking back now, I realize that something was happening. I was being taught again that important lesson about life: we are alone and the meager security we have created for ourselves will not last. This time pushed me over the line and I became very afraid. Worse yet, I was stuck inside this fear. I don't know why I didn't talk to anyone about it. I suppose I could have, and maybe someone even asked if I wanted to. However, when you are alone you tend to stay alone, and when you are carrying something large you just carry it until you collapse beneath it.

That day colored the rest of my childhood. I fully realized that I was not safe, and there was nothing I could do about it. The last of my innocence rode away in an ambulance on a warm summer afternoon. I had nothing to hold onto. Imagination was no longer an escape because I had seen that death makes everything I recognized as worthwhile go away. I was no longer able to swallow the religious chatter about the afterlife. Once you are really afraid of death the idea that you should just have faith and everything will be okay seems ludicrous.

I now felt profoundly isolated as well as deeply fearful. This fear became something that either terrorized me or that I somehow managed to distract myself from. I either experienced fear or wildly engaged in anything to keep it out of my awareness. My preference was to perform for attention and connection and do absolutely anything to avoid rejection. I got my share of attention, but it never amounted to much. The attention that did come was certainly not enough to make me feel safe again. The only choice I had was to perform faster and more frequently and hope that I could forget.

# Chapter Five
# Witnessing a Death

Life is relentless. No matter what the personal struggle, no matter how afraid you are, life will drag you along behind it if you refuse to move forward. I limped into my teenage years, fearful and grasping for a connection to someone or something that would make me feel safe. I moved from one disappointment to another more out of habit than anything else. As I look back at those years I am amazed at what a human being can get used to. Even the fear of death will become mundane after enough time. You go from fearing death specifically to being generally afraid all the time. The source fades into the background and fear itself becomes everything.

It was a late October Saturday, cold and damp. The weather was working its way toward an ice cold, almost raining mist. My mother was in the kitchen, and I was alone in another room playing Atari and focused on getting through the first level of a new game. I remember hearing a knock at the door and thinking to myself that a visitor during mealtime was odd. But I went on with my game, not listening to the conversation until I heard my mother say my name.

I walked into the kitchen and saw the sheriff's deputy standing in the doorway. He stared at the floor and looked as though he could hardly stand up. In rural Iowa, there is only one reason for the sheriff to appear at your home, looking the way he did. The moment you see him it's time to count heads, because whoever is missing isn't coming home. As soon as I saw the deputy, I knew that my father was gone. I simply waited for the words to come, which quietly, they did. "There's been an accident..."

The rest of that sentence hit me like a ball bat. I couldn't breathe or even stay on my feet. I dropped backward into the stairwell and my mother came to help me. I wanted to scream, but I couldn't even get my body to cooperate well enough to breathe. I started sucking in labored rasping breaths. My mother sat me on the stairs and moved on to check on my brothers. I sat there and hyperventilated until my vision got dark around the edges. I felt like I was looking out of a hole.

I don't know if I passed out. Maybe I just went away for a while. But whatever happened in that moment was a harbinger of the days ahead. When I came to, the house was filled with neighbors who had heard the news. They had come to start the vigil that death brings to every rural home it visits. I sat in the middle of all this with a sort of stunned incomprehension. I wasn't really thinking about anything because I couldn't any more. Whoever I was, whatever I was had vanished.

As if the first two lessons weren't enough, I had to learn again about the impermanence of safety, other people, and even myself. I now knew for certain that nothing could protect me. I would never be safe again. It only took a few moments before I asked the question that everyone gets around to asking, "why me?" Once I started down this road, the answers came quickly.

Whatever God was in charge of the universe had simply taken my father. I could no longer believe that there were reasons for things like this. Nothing would have explained it. My God had taken my father knowing full well I could scarcely tolerate a loss of that magnitude. There would never be a reason that made any sense. And right there everything I believed about Gods and men suddenly became empty. In that moment, I lost whatever meaning my life held was swallowed up by fear. Everything I was crumbled and I walked out the door into a cold October rain.

Several days passed and my mother, who tried to hold herself as well as the rest of us together, decided in very traditional fashion that we should view my father's body before he was cremated. I didn't really want to do this but I was told it was important and that if I didn't I would regret it. After all, it was the last time I would see my father. By this time the house was filled with family, and for whatever reason, they wanted this. I thought about it, and decided maybe they were right. I have never been more wrong.

His death certificate mentioned something like "Massive Head Trauma." This is the gentlest of euphemisms for what I saw that day. What should have been written on that form was: "A tractor ran over his head opening his skull and making his face unrecognizable." Someone had spent what must have been days using what looked like silly putty to put my father's head back together so that his family could look at him again. I am grateful for what they tried to do but at that moment I recognized the suit and little else.

My family stood around him talking about how peaceful he looked. Some of them actually made statements like, "It almost looks like him." What I saw was the last moments of a good man who deserved better from his world and his God. To work so hard for so little and then to have it end in what must have been a terrifying instant is just wrong. Did he scream or cry out? Did he suffer? Was he angry? I was.

As I am writing this I am crying. I cry because at 39 I can no longer bring a clear image of my father into my mind. I can recall a few memories of him at a distance or in profile. His living face has quite simply gone from me. But I have now, and I suspect I will always have, the full-color image of what was left of him that day. It makes me sad to think that as my memories of him continue to fade, I will see that image clearly, forever.

Given the normal tendency toward adolescent rebellion, all the elements were present for ugliness. I had been force fed all the fear and pain that I could stomach. God had clearly shown his indifference and possibly dislike for me. I began to feel as though I had been robbed of the life everyone else seemed to have. I became angry because what I once thought I was missing, I now knew had been taken from me. My isolation and fear were no longer coincidences or just bad luck. The only way a life could be this shitty was by design. I was now on the outside of the universe looking in, and God had placed me there.

Why anger you might ask, rather than diving into the mind-numbing depression beneath it? The easy answer is that as a young male, anger was my birthright, but the real reason is different. When someone you love dies in an accident, you or some member of your family will quite likely find themselves in a room with a small group of attorneys. Insurance, workman's compensation, and self-protection make this inevitable. It is during this meeting that you find out exactly what your loved one is worth.

The attorneys will talk at length about depositions, settlements, witnesses and trial. The conversation will likely go on for months. You will be exposed to attorneys representing the opposition who are very sorry for your loss but seems willing to blame what happened on anyone but those they work for. The blaming happens not because it has anything to do with truth but because it has everything to do with money. Unless you have been unfortunate enough to have gone through something like this, you may have never stopped to consider that your loved one can actually be reduced to a price per pound.

We were not wealthy enough to mount much of a legal case. In these situations you realize quickly that the life of those you love is only worth as much as you already have in the checkbook. The total worth of my father's life was somewhere in the neighborhood of $70,000, of which the lawyers took a third. Not even 40 years old, with a wife and three children, and all parties involved decided that $70,000 should just about cover the damage. I wonder how my mother felt when they told her that this was as good as it would get.

Having said all this I want you to understand that I'm not crying sour grapes. My situation is no different than the countless people that have experienced this ugliness before me, and since. I'm not whining because we should have been given more money. The issue here is that this process successfully minimized and then all but denied the value of my father's life and by default the lives of myself and my family.

By the time all this was over, whatever ties I had to the world around me were gone. Even the members of my family began to move away from one another. We should have come together. My mother tried, and I think we wanted to. But alone people don't really know how to do this in the best of times, let alone at a time like this. So we all did what we had to do to keep our own heads above the water.

I felt as though events outside my control had forcibly ejected me from the world other people happily occupied. I was completely overwhelmed by these feelings until some internal fuse blew; then I couldn't feel anything but anger and fear. Even the natural world that had sustained me when I was a child now meant nothing. I felt no sense of connection to anything or anyone. For me to feel anything at all, it had to be intense, loud, fast, and hard.

I could see and hear the world. I could even interact with it to some extent. But I couldn't really feel anything that didn't smash itself against me. Human beings, and particularly young people, need to feel a sense of connection to people and the world. The immediate physical sensation of belonging and contact with the world we live in is the most important form of nourishment for our deepest being. Without it, we are at risk of emotionally and spiritually starving to death. I didn't know it at the time but I was about to begin what amounted to a hunger strike.

Dissociation is God's gift to humans who can't tolerate what is happening to them. Built into our psyche is an ancient ability to step away from whatever is happening right now. The further we step back the less we feel. Almost anything is bearable if you step back far enough into some dark corner of yourself. It's like being on the other side of a window. The real you sits huddled far back in the corner of your head and sees the events of your life play out before your eyes. You don't actually participate in anything. You just observe it. From this place of refuge the important parts of you are safe. Nothing can harm you anymore.

Dissociation is an outstanding way to generate a sense of safety and security in daily life. You keep the real being inside tucked safely away and you develop a kind of false self that moves around in the world. It's like putting brand new siding on an abandoned house full of matches and cans of gasoline. It looks just like every other house but the interior design is something altogether different.

The downside, at least for me, was that dissociation is also the most desperate form of loneliness. I had little human contact of any significance, at least none I could feel. I had found somewhere safe to hide, but by remaining there I would eventually starve and die. I didn't die right away because the process takes time. I became a tightly wrapped ball of anger that slowly started to become more hostile. I was desperately lonely and afraid, and no matter what I did I felt only more loneliness and fear. I started to aim my anger at those I wanted to feel but couldn't. This, of course, made me more isolated, and I crawled further into myself. I starved, and I became more unhappy and self-destructive.

The distinct impression that death is just around the corner, combined with depression, breeds a passive form of suicidal thinking. I wasn't out there leaping in front of moving vehicles, but I was definitely playing in the road. All the time I was hoping to find some way out of the corner I had backed myself into, but

I don't think I really believed I would find it. I think I hoped that death would finally catch up with me, and the whole thing would be over.

After high school, I had several unremarkable jobs and then a stint in the military. This taught me very quickly that in addition to being angry, I have a problem with authority. Well, not so much with authority as with unfairness and hypocrisy. It is the hypocrisy of power that I have no tolerance for. I already knew I had a problem with authority, but I was amazed to learn how bad it really was.

I had seen too much hypocrisy and uninterested blindness in my youth. Small towns do not have more hypocrisy than other places, but these worlds are very small and the smell is more redolent. Watching and listening to people tell me that they were doing what was right and then seeing them doing something else always angered me. This is particularly true of people who have a responsibility to care for those around them. I think anger in the face of the hypocrisy of power is the genesis of apathy in all young people. If I can't act like others do or make sense of what they do, my only choice is to stop caring.

I am not overly ethical nor do I see myself as some kind of standard for others to live up to. In fact, I'm not terribly honest with most of the people around me. I think this is the habit of a child who always needed others to approve of him. At any rate, even though I still don't feel I owe anyone honesty, I know I have to be honest with myself. I learned very early that the admonition to "always be honest and never lie" is more an effort to control someone than a necessary element of good character. In the end it is yourself that you cannot lie to.

Honesty is an element of trust that emerges between people, once it is earned. If you are going to tell me to "be honest" you better make sure you're being honest with yourself first. If you're telling me to be honest and I see you saying one thing and doing another than I know you're more interested in control than honesty. Honesty like other pillars of good character is generally a code word for control and conformity. My unbridled distain for today's character fascists, mixed with what I feel to be a very appropriate cynicism, makes me suspicious of anyone who suggests that they are anything other than a deeply flawed human being who has no business telling someone else what to do, think, or say.

To those of you who are convinced that you are a good person and see the judgment of others as a necessary activity I would offer the following: I know you are in pain. I know your life is not as good as you portray. I know you have deep wounds that you pretend don't exist. I know you have huge blind spots in your image of who you are. I know you want to be bad in one or two very important ways. I know that in many ways you do things you say you don't do. I know you do the very things you are publicly opposed to. I know there is a part of yourself you hate. I know you lie even if you say you don't. I know you are not a moral or ethical pillar no matter what you say to the contrary. I know your "character" is flawed in a way that does not entitle you to say anything to anyone about their "character". You know what? All this is fine with me. I am willing to accept you exactly as you are. But I will demand the same courtesy from you and don't try to sell me load of shit. I'll keep a close watch on my stuff if you do the same.

After my foray into military service I decided to try college and, surprisingly, I did quite well. The real reason for my success at college was that I was involved with real teachers like T.S. Chia, Jack Hill, and Tom Gilbert. There is a distinction between teachers and professors. The academic world has many professors but only a few teachers. Professors need to be seen in a particular way and need you to think and feel in a particular way. Usually their way. These needs are more important than anything having to do with their students and the growth of these students. This approach sits in clear opposition to that of a teacher.

For a teacher, the student's dignity and growth is always first. The teacher invites and challenges the student to grow and become something different. He or she doesn't manipulate or control because it's not necessary. The genius of a teacher is the genius of the invitation. They present it in such a way that it is irresistible. You learn and grow not because you're forced to. You do it because you can't help it. This is what it is to learn. I am forever in favor of teachers and learning, and I have little time or tolerance for professors and education.

Graduate school was a mixed blessing filled with several fine teachers and a few noteworthy professors who remain to this day examples of what I do not want to be. Teachers like Shelly Boughner, Grace Mims, and Spencer Davis taught me a great deal about how to be who you are and in the process, offer acceptance and compassion to others. But more important than this, they practiced as they preached and accepted me for who I was. This allowed me to look more closely at who I am. This was the first intensely honest look I had ever taken at myself and, as you can imagine, the exercise was fraught with pain as well as joy.

Graduate work in psychology is, for most students, a rich exercise in self-discovery and self-delusion. I was no exception. I studied the theory and practice of psychotherapy, went to psychotherapy weekly and worked hard to understand what was inside me. After years of such work not much had changed. Yes, I had less conflict in my life. Yes, I behaved and functioned differently. But the things that mattered, the fear and anger; they never changed. I had just started to act again. Now, I was acting like I was normal. I remember a professor telling me that acting different was the first step to being different. I'd been an actor all my life and I knew that acting only makes you better at acting. If you mistake acting and pretending for change or worse growth than in the end you have nothing.

I suspected then, and I believe today, that the deeper, more honest existence inside me, and inside all people, is impervious to therapy of any kind. Therapy changes the surface, the outer layers, and makes them more acceptable. But the very real mystery at the center of our being seems to remain untouched. Psychotherapy of any kind is only rarely able to reach what we really are. If the problems are on the surface, in the outer layers, it works great. If not, it appears to accomplish little or nothing. So I admitted to myself that psychology and psychotherapy did not hold the answers I was looking for and tried to think of what I was going to do next. I was considering leaving school when a phone call came that changed the direction of my life.

# Chapter Six
# When the Student is Ready

My good friend and former teacher, Dr. Tom Gilbert, called me unexpectedly one October afternoon. He said that a local priest and poet, was coming to the philosophy of fine arts class that evening to give a lecture. Based on what he knew about this man, Tom felt I would enjoy the talk and he urged me to come. I had school that evening but I wasn't enjoying the class that much. In fact, I wasn't enjoying anything that much. I thought about it for a whole second and a half before I told him I would be there.

As I recall, I arrived late, and when I walked into the room Fr. Frahm had already started his lecture. He stopped talking and looked at me. I said, "I'm sorry for interrupting." He smiled broadly and said, "Please, sit." My first encounter with him consisted of listening as he lectured to a room full of undergraduate philosophy and English students about poetry and the contemplative life. If you had been watching that evening from the other side of the room, I am sure the whole thing would have looked completely unremarkable. But nothing could have been further from the truth.

Fr. Frahm spent most of the evening talking at length about me and the interesting things I had been doing over the last decade. It was as if someone had told him my history, my thoughts and the things that scared me. He went on to suggest very simply that I had been looking at my life the wrong way. He said that my fear and anger were the result of a longing to connect with something, rather than a problem I should run from. He said that most of our behavior, good, bad and irrelevant, is actually in service of this longing to connect with something larger than ourselves. Because inside us we know that only by connecting with something larger than ourselves will we ever be complete. The absence of this connection causes a sense of lack and inside sense of lack we become afraid, among other things. Most importantly, however, he said that only by letting go of who and what we think we are will we ever connect with something larger than ourselves, and find peace.

He went on to describe how we will go almost anywhere if it promises something beyond the narrow, fear-ridden confines of our isolated mind and the self we think we are. If we cannot find this sense of connection or we become separated from it beyond our individual tolerance, our search will become increasingly intense and desperate. Until finally, we give up the search altogether and collapse or explode. The circumstances, nature, and extent of our search make up most of the phenomena we usually refer to as mental illness, interpersonal problems, addiction, and life difficulties.

He defined this longing not as a mental health issue, behavioral problem, or character flaw but as a process of becoming. We feel the absence of a larger consciousness that is by definition divine. If we look at life, both beautiful and problematic, as an inherent drive to return to the divine center of everything, there is no failure. If all roads lead to Rome, then there are no wrong turns. There is only a journey you have not yet finished. From this prospective, problems and suffering not only have meaning but they become a vehicle for creative growth and revelation.

Fr. Frahm stated clearly that human suffering is real. It is a natural part of life, and for the most part unavoidable. He felt that we suffer not because of our longing but because (this is the important part) we misunderstand the longing. Our failure to understand is best represented by the manner in which we are trying to cope. We feel the absence of contact with the Divine, we become confused and afraid, and we begin to grasp at things to fill the emptiness inside us.

This course of action can only lead to more longing, more grasping, and a more vivid sense of the absence at the center of your life. Fr. Frahm suggested that contemplation of this absence and a sense of wonder about the Divine were more useful and productive avenues to travel. Since what you long for is contact with the divine, Fr. Frahm felt that this made the issues and problems revolving around this longing, spiritual problems. He felt that when you approach spiritual problems from a contemplative prospective, with the longing for God as your focus, you have no choice but to grow and become something more.

I had never heard anything like this before, and I was unsure what to make of it. I struggled to believe what he was saying because my natural tendency is toward a healthy skepticism. However, I felt something familiar begin to emerge from inside me. As I listened to him, I recalled my memories and feelings from the pastures and fields of my childhood. I remembered what it was like to feel connected to something and then I realized that what I had felt connected to, was God.

How could I not be curious now? According to Fr. Frahm, my life, problematic as it was, had been a pilgrimage, as all lives are. Not only was I not headed down the wrong path, I had been moving toward the answer I wanted all along. I needed to know more.

This sounds simple as I relay it here. Perhaps to you this kind of information is common knowledge. But during that two-hour lecture Fr. Frahm gave me a way to understand myself and my life that I had never considered. More importantly though, he sat at the front of that room not knowing me from Adam, and somehow managed to issue an invitation that caused something inside me to respond. He had taken my understanding of my life and turned it on its head. It was as if I'd been in prison for years and suddenly someone told me that the door had been unlocked all along.

I don't know if the others in the class had this experience. If they did I wasn't aware of it. I have, on several occasions, asked myself why I was there and why I responded the way I did. I never asked Fr. Frahm what his thoughts were on this question, but I know what he would have said: "When the student is ready, the teacher will come."

It was not that he believed himself to be my teacher and I his student. He only believed that people ripen throughout their lives and become ready to harvest. If you can see what is real and you are ready to harvest yourself, the universe quite often will put what you need right in front of you. Each human life has multiple opportunities to harvest. If you're not ready this time, you simply wait until the next opportunity. But, if you don't bring in today's harvest today, you will not have access to this specific harvest again. Harvests are cyclical, and there will be others, but that particular one disappears forever.

Because we harvest only what we understand, it is common that other people are involved in this process. Deep understanding usually emerges from relationship with someone or something rather than in isolation. Frequently this other person arrives as a teacher of some sort. This teacher is not a miracle or some extraordinary event; it's just a part of the way life works, no more and no less. When we are able to clearly see the teachers in our daily lives and our boundaries permit it, we can harvest who we are. If we do not see clearly, if we hold too many boundaries, we can't harvest anything.

I had been ripening on the vine for some time but my perception of myself and my life prevented me from seeing what was real. Inside my mind, fear and anger about my past prevented me from being free of it. It owned me. I was a prisoner of my own history. Then this man came along and told me that my prison existed only in my mind. My life had been a movement toward something larger than my individual self and its ideas about the world. As it turns out it was the fear I carried and the anger I clung to that had been preparing me for what I longed for.

I had heard people say the things Fr. Frahm was saying before. There had never been a shortage of pundits and counselors who were willing, for the price of their time, to give me all the instructions I would ever need on how to live. This type of talk had little impact on me, and part of me suspected that Fr. Frahm's words would ultimately be empty as well. Even after such a strong response I waited for the other shoe to drop for quite some time. But the shoe never dropped. There was something different about Fr. Frahm.

I no longer remember exactly what he said that evening, but by the end something within me started to change. As I look back on it, it was something akin to a baptism, my baptism. It did not come from outside me, and no third party or religious entity could claim responsibility for it. I freely chose to sit within that moment and submit to it. Fr. Frahm had simply opened a door and I chose to walk through it.

Baptism is not some external God granting you X, Y, and Z. Baptism is a moment when, because of a choice you make, something wakes up inside you. It's nothing new; quite likely you have felt it before. You recognize that you are part of something much larger than your individual self and you realize that it was suffering that brought you to where you are. When this happens you are changed and you see a new world in which there is only One thing, and you are part of it.

The class ended and I sat in a kind of happy stupor. I walked up to Fr. Frahm and tried to tell him how much I enjoyed what he said. I no longer remember exactly what I said, but I think I managed to say something understandable. He looked me over for a moment, probably trying to assess my sincerity or purpose. Once he satisfied himself, he invited me out for coffee.

By the time I got to the restaurant I no longer felt overwhelmed to the point of babbling. Now I had questions. He sat for several hours and devoted himself to my concerns. My questions that evening were of the "How do I know you're not full of shit?" variety. To his credit he answered them all, some with compassion and some with fierceness and some with the mischief of a child. This conversation only made me more curious. At the end of the evening, he shook my hand and said that if I wanted to talk further I was welcome to give him a call, and we would work something out.

I left the restaurant and drove home. I felt a sense of hopefulness for the first time in many years. As a result, I spent the next six days arguing with myself over when I should call. I ultimately waited a week because I did not want to appear too eager and somehow make him uncomfortable. Or worse yet, appear creepy or bizarre. When I called, he said he was happy to hear from me and looked forward to having me at his home.

When I arrived he showed me to the dinning room, where home-made pie and ice tea, were waiting. It appeared, delightfully, that it was his practice to feed the stomach as well as the soul. As curious as I was about learning more from him, I never turn down pie. And every time I came to his home after that it was the same. He loved to engage in this strange type of unassuming table fellowship. I would arrive and sit down, and we would begin to eat and talk.

There is something very human about the act of eating together. It isn't quite the food, and it isn't quite the people, but somewhere inside the ease of a simple meal, if it's done properly, you can return to the ground of what you are. You can just be there without the need to appear as something other than what you really are. The act of eating together seems to make it easier to be honest about what you think and feel. Over time, the simplicity of this fellowship allowed me to drop my defenses and just be with another person.

I don't believe Fr. Frahm was manipulating me, but he definitely knew something I didn't. What he knew was that taking those first steps and beginning to shed the outer coverings of the self is difficult but absolutely necessary. And, more importantly, it has to be a choice that you make without any expectations of return or gain. In other words, you can't do it with the expectation of being fixed, cured or otherwise cared for. If you carry the expectation that the other person is going to fix you than all your choices cease to be real and become a form of manipulation.

The more frequently I chose to honestly be who I am, the more sacred and safe the environment seemed. Over time, this process became a ritual, it became a sacrament, but it was a sacrament that gave no absolution and no promises. But it did do something more important, it contained and nurtured love. I slowly began to learn a very important lesson; that with love there is little need of anything else.

It would be easy to see this encounter as similar to a psychotherapeutic process, but this would be wrong on so many levels. There was no agenda, no expectation of return and no rehashing of days or years. He never offered anything neutral or professional. He gave no feedback, reflection, or interpretation. It was simply two people sitting together—one of them real and alive, able to love himself and everything else, the other wanting to do the same.

As I think about it now, what he did was the exact opposite of psychotherapy. When you entered into relationship with Fr. Frahm you had to choose to be there with absolutely no expectations of being fixed or helped. He made it fairly clear that you have to help yourself. He never took responsibility for anyone's problems or solutions. He just sat with you and loved you. And somehow, everything else took care of itself.

This type of relationship was Fr. Frahm's preferred element, and within it, he thrived. He took two pieces of pie, a batch of cookies or a sunny day and transformed them into something that sustained the human mind and heart. It was a sacrament that invited me to love myself and gave me the choice of loving the one who sat with me. I didn't realize it at first, but these were necessary steps if I was to find my way to what I longed for.

Our fellowship and sacrament were not particularly religious. The words Jesus or God rarely entered the conversation for many months. I can only say that for me it was more significant than any religious sacrament ever was or probably ever will be. Its importance rested in the fact that it was not about me requesting love from God, whatever God is. It was about me learning to love me. The first and most important thing I learned is this: Love for yourself is where all love has to start, because without it you are lost. Fr. Frahm must have told me a thousand times, "If you can't love yourself, you can't love God."

I learned to love myself by watching, listening, and feeling someone else choose to love me. He loved himself and he chose to love me no matter what

I said or did. And in return he wanted nothing. If I chose to love him that was good but it was of little consequence. His love was constant regardless. In one of his poems, the Sonnets to David he says as much, "Beyond my love's long reach you cannot go." So, I watched, I practiced, and I learned. Once I was able to love myself, I could allow someone else to love me and only then could I begin to move toward what I longed for.

Many of you know a person(s) who, if they fix their eyes on you, can look directly into your internal world. Fr. Frahm was one of those people. He had a long gentle face that was quick and expressive. I did not, for quite some time, find this ability to look into me particularly comforting. Nor did Fr. Frahm go out of his way to coddle me or protect me. My life was always my life. Nothing was minimized or forgiven. Many of our conversations were quite difficult and painful for me. As I think back, I'm sure that the only reason I could endure the process for so many years was that when I sat with him, I was never beyond love.

His secret, I have come to realize, was that he made every effort to love everything around him without judgment. He might not have liked it or approved of it, but that never stopped him from loving something or someone. And he knew that the only way to honestly and deeply love was without judgment. Again, he may not have liked something, but as the end of the day it didn't matter. The only one keeping it alive was the one who carried it. He taught me repeatedly that the idea of hating the sin but loving the sinner was, for human beings, largely impossible.

Most people in the helping professions do not think that loving people is wise or useful. They suggest that this is somehow confusing, harmful or dangerous. And I suppose that inside the manufactured relationships of the helping profession this is probably the case. Rather, these folks opt for ideas like presence, empathy or compassion. The problem is that this leaves you with nothing but a half-baked combination of eye contact, minimal verbal encouragers, centered breathing and empathetic statements to attempt contact with the mystery of the human heart. Fr. Frahm did not believe these were bad or harmful ideas, he just knew that without love they wouldn't take most of us very far. He believed that the choice to love, and then to act, was the only thing that would bring growth.

When you choose to love everything without judgment the boundaries that separate and isolate the individual from every other thing begin to fade. This allows you to step outside the everyday duality that most of us inhabit. Duality is the black and white world we live in each day where everything is either "this" or "that." Life is either good, or bad, exciting or boring, correct or incorrect. Duality is the everyday boundaried life.

Fr. Frahm said that many people chose to love everything or want to do so. It is the judgment issue that causes the real problem. Much of what Fr. Frahm taught was about judgment; the judgment of self and then others. It is this judgment that prevents us from ever coming into contact with God. He knew that human beings just don't want to give this up. There are many reasons for this and none of them are about love. According to Fr. Frahm judgment was about playing God.

Love is not attached to "this position" or "that belief" and in fact love is able and willing to hold everything. This is important because when boundaries begin to fade and we can hold multiple truths, something new can emerge. This newness integrates many truths and, as it does, you can move beyond them. Our growth changes what we are in this world, and takes us toward the divine at the center of everything.

Again, love cannot be empathy or compassion. Though there is nothing wrong with either of these choices, they are almost always manufactured fallacies. Love is a state in which everything, good or bad, can exist, and with some effort, be accepted, or at least tolerated and given a place. This process allows us to see reality a little more clearly and we no longer need to control everything around us or steer the world in a desired direction. Without this burden there is no reason to hold onto our boundaries and illusions to be secure.

Fr. Frahm simply sat with me, but he did it with love. This experience was different than anything I had previously encountered. He experienced everything I said or did. He was not distracted or in any way unavailable. He had nothing to gain or prove, and strangely he had no agenda for me. When I sat with him, I got this strange feeling that there was nothing to stick to. Because Fr. Frahm was centered in himself, he needed nothing from me. So there was no way to play games or manipulate him to gain anything.

All of the normal qualities of the individual that we read in one another and work to spin and manipulate were absent or at least minimized. He could not be influenced or controlled to any great degree. If I tried to control him in some fashion he would endure it for awhile and then politely confront me with what I was doing. Fr. Frahm was completely free from me and everything else around him. This placed me in a position where I was also free of him and over time I had to learn to accept this.

Everyone's ability to love is different and Fr. Frahm's ability was immense. It was like standing in front of the Grand Canyon and immediately recognizing the reality of your size and place. And when he was sitting with you, he was love. It was as if there were no conflicts, doubts, fears, or anger in him anywhere, at least none that mattered. With no agenda to hide and few boundaries to diminish him, he could love anyone. Fr. Frahm loved you because you were you, and as he was found of saying, "you are worth loving."

I am not the only one who received this gift. During the time I knew him, there was always someone coming to see him. One person left and another arrived. The frequency of this parade of people was often amazing. It lasted from morning to midnight some days. They came for the same reasons I did, to feel loved and in this love to grow.

With the benefit of time, I understand him and his love somewhat differently now. I knew Fr. Frahm for a decade, sat with him during joy and sorrow, and then ultimately helped him die. The person I understand today is everything I felt in the beginning but it has become much simpler. His love was outside or beyond human suffering, mine or his own. It was a boundless love that could hold anger, rage, shame, and the tender parts of the human heart.

Fr. Frahm never denied anything in himself and he never denied anything in another person. With courage, he accepted it all and with this he became more authentic and creative. He was beyond any boundary or limitation. Not because he transcended anything but because he lived at the boundary. He loved his boundaries when he discovered them and he didn't reject them. He accepted what took him there and the mystery that was beyond it. He was in love with the mystery of the boundary and this kept him on the frontier of his life where creativity and revelation were everywhere. Fr. Frahm was fully alive.

# Chapter Seven
# The Teacher will Come

Over time, my initial questions and concerns became less pressing and we moved on to other things. We would often talk for hours about the varied ideas and subjects that interested us. I recall that education, science, poetry, and literature where common topics of conversation. You only needed to sit with Fr. Frahm for a short time before you became aware that he spoke impeccably good English. And by impeccable I mean perfect.

He wrote and spoke with a grammar, structure, and vocabulary that suggested he was well-educated with some type of English influence. A friend of mine who was a doctoral student in English remarked upon leaving his first meeting with Fr. Frahm, "Now that's a man who knows how to handle his participles." Fr. Frahm's communication had a precision and intensity that was impossible to miss and somewhat unnerving.

But his way of speaking could also be quite humorous. He loved to laugh and joke and he would, with some regularity, curse. His English accent, combined with the fact that he placed a lowly common word in the midst of the most pristine and educated company, produced a disjointed and shocking effect. The well-spoken holy man would curse, and I would have to stifle my laughter. I learned from him that you don't make an impression with bad words. You make an impression with the words you place around them. It is one thing to be called an ass. It is quite another to be called an unconscionable, truculent ass.

Fr. Frahm was gracious and well-mannered to a fault and he loved to cook and entertain. If you stopped to see him, no matter what the time, he would almost certainly offer you something to eat and drink. If he didn't have a little nosh available he would get up and prepare something to get you by. I was always struck with the importance he placed on little things when he was taking care of his guests. I remember one occasion when he offered me raspberry pie and would not allow me to eat until he had found a chocolate stick, and placed it, just so, in the top of the pie. To eat it otherwise would have been unthinkable. The importance of this gesture was so striking that I felt guilty removing the stick so I could eat what remained. All of this contributed to the sense that something special was happening.

I came to understand years later that he treated all of his guests as though they were God in disguise. This was an idea Fr. Frahm spoke about often. He loved to tell stories about God arriving at the home of someone who was unaware of his identity. These stories suggested, and Fr. Frahm believed, that true test of our love for others rested in how we treated strangers and guests. He told me repeatedly that how you treated a stranger was how you would treat God. At Fr. Frahm's house, God, whether he wanted it or not, would get his chocolate stick "just so."

I am aware that my description of Fr. Frahm can sound too perfect or even border on magical. Perhaps it is. I think my perception of him is similar to what people may have felt like when Gandhi, Buddha, Jesus or some other great teacher reached out to them. All great teachers reach out from a different place than the rest of us. And it is amazing to be on the receiving end of this. All you can do is sit and feel overwhelmed by love. Suddenly, while you just stand there, you are lovable. Your existence has value. With the realization of this gift it is easier to love yourself, and then, others. In spite of all this, he was simply my friend and a friend to countless others. His teaching was no great project or official undertaking. I, like everyone else, just came. We came because he loved us, and soon we found ourselves loving him.

Initially, it was a lot of work to be with Fr. Frahm. The experience of interacting with him was different than anything I had known before. It was much more intense than normal interaction and also much simpler. Fr. Frahm didn't have shallow conversation. Speaking with him often produced the sense of being cognitively, emotionally and spiritually naked. This sense was at the same time, frightening and wonderfully free. It was like being completely known by someone. You were really seen by another person and you were valued because you were you.

This sense of being known could at times be too much to take. Interacting with Fr. Frahm had an intensity to it that is hard to describe. He would often meet me at the door and begin to talk about the exact sentence we had left off with the day before. It was obvious that what I said was important to him and he had spent his time contemplating it long after I went home. Any conversation with Fr. Frahm was serious business.

This constant intensity combined with the sense of always being seen and known produced an immense vulnerability and then a deep exhaustion. Normal people are not equipped to step into a situation where there is no way to evade responsibility for being who and what you are. The mental aerobics necessary to tolerate this kind of exchange will leave you feeling as though you just ran a marathon. And some days, I have to admit, I was very happy to be away from him.

But speaking with him was simple as well. Fr. Frahm was a rare human being in that he did not need to see his emotional reflection in those around him. Because of this, he was free to meet everyone who came to him honestly and authentically. For most people, even on Fr. Frahm's worst day, this type of encounter was so liberating that he or she was able to become something different than they had been a moment before. They became more loving or more understanding or more themselves. As they began to change and grow they could handle their own difficulties more effectively. This was his idea all along. He did not feel compelled to fix or save you. His only wish was to offer love, without judgment.

I, like everyone else, came to Fr. Frahm wanting something. Some wanted to be his friend. Others wanted to be a better father, mother, husband or wife, a better lover, a happier person. The list goes on and on. He encountered us all as individuals and in relationship with him he invited us to be something more or something different. In most cases, we were simply invited to be who we really were. He invited you not into a therapeutic rehashing of your life, but rather into a place where you realized that none of that stuff was of any real importance. All you needed to do to be free was to become who and what you really were.

Fr. Frahm interacted in a way that invited you to be exactly what you were. Because he didn't shy away from what was inside him, and he didn't hide it from you, it was suddenly much easier to be whatever you were. He could gently encourage, yet leave you free to be whom and what you needed and wanted to be. Whatever that was he blessed it and loved it. Since he had little need to judge who you are, you were always lovable.

When you are young, it is your parents' job to witness your life and your experiences and then name them and give them value. As they do this, the events of your life, and the contents of yourself, become real and acquire meaning. Once they are seen and acknowledged by another, they can no longer be an idea or something abstract that can be easily denied. It is this process that solidifies much of who we are.

Parents are also supposed to name and accept their child's personhood as it emerges. You look at a developing being, see it for what it is, and name it as good and worthwhile. This process of naming a life and accepting it stabilizes and gives form to a young self. This same process is also necessary for older people who missed something along the way. Fr. Frahm knew this and so he would work to name and accept your being and then he would love it, all the while making it seem like the only correct thing to do. As he did this, he helped to stabilize and give form to older selves that struggled with some aspect of their lives.

This was his role as a teacher. He sat with those who came to him and accepted their entire being, even the parts they didn't like, until they began to have the courage to love those parts as well. Once there is love, transcendence comes in the form of not caring as much about many of the things that once bothered you. Only by loving who you are right now, does the guilt of the past and the fear of the future fade away. Fr. Frahm did not spend his time focusing on the next life, but on another way to live the one you have right now.

Part of what he used to accomplish this task was poetry. All of his poetry was, in some significant way, about acceptance and love. His poems developed out of the relationship of his being with the world around him. When he read poetry, his own or someone else's, (which he often did), he read with the purpose of inviting the listener to step closer to whom and what they really were. He invited you to hear an idea resonate in your heart without being compelled to do, say, or think anything about it. For Fr. Frahm, the invitation and opportunity to be authentically ourselves was more important than the poem itself or any message it might convey. He knew that if you focus too much on the words it is likely that you will miss something important. You will miss that millisecond of oneness that you had to reason away or ignore, believing it childish, strange, or worthless. You will miss what is real.

Much of Fr. Frahm's poetry is a roadmap of sorts that invites you to be present inside the moment you currently inhabit. The poem is offered to you in a manner that invites you to be authentically awake with it and in it. He believed too much in the freedom of the individual to force acceptance, love or anything else on you or manipulate you into it. You had to make a choice for yourself. He simply showed it to you and invited you in. If you went where you were invited, you might begin to suspect that there must be something to the whole "love" thing after all.

To illustrate what I mean, and what I think Fr. Frahm meant by acceptance and love, I offer you one of his poems written in 2002. It is a description of what happened when he encountered a vacant lot.

<u>Vacant Lots</u>
This vacant lot's not vacant
for those with eyes to see;
its sunflowers more than satisfy
the meadowlarks and me.
Consider, too, the sumac:
in autumn sun it glows
as foil to yellow goldenrod
more carmine than the rose.
Winter—a quiet corner
where few but children go
to trace the deer and rabbit tracks
through democratic snow.

Here springs the glad remittance
for chilling April showers

> when dandelions far outshine
> tame pretentious flowers.
> As expectations deafen
> and prejudices blind,
> so preferences pauperize
> the closed and idle mind.

Inside Fr. Frahm's personal presence, there existed a center of gravity that pulled everything toward it. His presence could literally be felt and if he wished to he could reach out and touch you with it. You need only have entered one or two rooms with him to understand that people reacted to him, strongly. It was this immense personal presence that enabled him to change the lives of those around him. The love that emanated from him was something you could reject but not escape. Although his personal presence was something of a mystery, the center that it was organized around was a little more visible.

Having spent countless hours with Fr. Frahm and having watched him interact with so many different people, I quickly realized that in some important way, the center of Fr. Frahm's presence was made up of the emotional pain that he held. If you spent any time with him at all you recognized that he was no stranger to pain, emotional or physical. And I think, like myself, many of us shared the sense that he carried a pain so severe and so deep that it frightened and fascinated us at the same time.

I know from conversations with other people that came to see Fr. Frahm that they visited him primarily to know that no matter what was happening to them, they could carry on. They came to realize that he had completely absorbed and accepted an enormous amount of pain and suffering. You just knew that when it came to pain, he had gone further than the rest of us. And just being physically close to him, allowed you to carry your burden another day. And knowing this, we also realized that we could never carry whatever it was he carried, and that only made us care about him more.

Fr. Frahm had what our culture euphemistically calls a "difficult childhood'. His birth mother put him up for adoption and his adopted parents, although basically decent people, were also abusive. These initial difficulties made him vulnerable to more severe problems as he grew to adulthood. The older man I knew still suffered from wounds he received as a child and was condemned to carry many of them to his death. This pain may not have mattered to him, but it had by no means gone away.

Fr. Frahm's ability to recognize and compassionately touch the suffering of others originated in his own familiarity with pain and suffering. His understanding and acceptance of others was born in a child that had experienced physical and emotional pain at the hands of those who were supposed to love. And more importantly this pain taught him that he was unwanted and unlovable. He learned these lessons well and as he grew, he went on to hurt himself.

Fr. Frahm spoke very little about his childhood during most of the time I knew him. If he shared something specific it was usually done to teach something specific. It seemed he only gave from this pain when he was very certain of the effect it would have. At first I thought he might have been protecting the rest of us from the ugliness of his life. Now however, I think he was really protecting himself from our pity. I also believe that this vagueness about his past was a kind of teaching. Fr. Frahm was suggesting that your past had little importance. Most people think they are their past, Fr. Frahm on the other hand, was not his.

Toward the end of his life however, he began to talk to me, in frightening detail, about his memories of childhood. What he had once intentionally hidden from me now pored out of a frail, sick man. He described his parents as people who had been hurt themselves and had grown to be angry. Even in the midst of his own pain, his first thoughts where of acceptance. From there however he described a mother who couldn't control her tongue and often spoke only to relieve her anger and frustration by hurting him. It was the same laundry list of stories that I had heard from every abused child I had ever worked with. In these stories the child is always used to relieve someone else's pain. Fr. Frahm described her as wicked and in spite of all the damage he never rejected her. He only said that frequently he had great difficulty loving her, and he acknowledged that she had difficulty loving him.

His descriptions of his father were more frightening. Fr. Frahm identified him as an abused child who was so full of rage he could scarcely contain it. He was quick to strike and seemed to never tire of doing so. If he was particularly inclined, he would use whatever object happened to be at hand. I remember the afternoon when Fr. Frahm described the unique sound that a 2 x 4 piece of lumber makes when it is broken across your back. In the next breath he spoke of a different sound. He talked of the weeks he sat next to his father as he was suffering a horribly painful death from brain cancer. Many sounds haunted Fr. Frahm into his old age. The worst I'm sure was the awful sucking sound made by his father's drainage tubes.

In his youth, Fr. Frahm was constantly troubled by the question of why his own people didn't want him. This was an issue he was much more open about and he seemed to almost want to know what other people thought. I don't know for certain, but I firmly believe he went as far as trying to find his birth mother. Before he died he showed me several documents he had requested earlier in life concerning his adoption. I suspect he searched for her because he was very certain about where his birth mother had come from and what has happening in that place at the time of his conception.

At the end of the day however, he knew he had been given away by his first family, and felt he was unwelcome in his second. This and the abuse he suffered insured he spent much of his youth believing that something was wrong with him and that he was not worth loving. His adoption had made him vulnerable to his adoptive parents, and they had made him vulnerable to just about anything or anyone.

There was not one significant relationship, particularly with women, that was untouched by what emerged from his childhood. The events of his early adulthood appear to be a direct result of his own deep sense of pain and the anger that grew from it. Before I give you a few details about his life, it is important to remember that the point of Fr. Frahm's story, in fact the point of his whole life, was that one can, with effort, transcend pain and suffering.

I feel compelled at this point to address the word transcendence. It is used a great deal in today's world, most frequently without real understanding or in circumstances where it doesn't belong. When I say transcendence, I am not suggesting that Fr. Frahm had reached some mystical level of consciousness. Transcendence does not imply that people live beyond or above those around them. In reality, it does not make human life much different. The same problems remain. The same challenges exist. Transcendence suggests that people have the same difficulties and feel the same things everyone else feels but they don't understand them in the same way. We find transcendence in a place just outside the duality of our daily lives where joys, ideas, and problems exist but are seen primarily through love and embraced rather than feared and rejected. All the baggage is there, it just doesn't matter as much.


As a young man, Fr. Frahm was intelligent and he did quite well in grammar school. His parents, who had little formal education themselves, were for some reason willing to indulge their son's gift. When he moved on to high school, he played numerous instruments in the band and participated in choir, drama, and many other leadership activities. High school held for him a modicum of happiness because during the four years he attended he did not have to live at home. The school in his hometown was not seen as an adequate preparation for college, and as Fr. Frahm continued to show great academic promise he was allowed to travel some 15 miles away to the county seat where he would board and attend high school. The sheer luck of being academically gifted had finally removed him from a hostile and often abusive environment.

This decision reflects well on his parents. All farm families depend to some extent upon their children to help them forge a growing business. In Fr. Frahm's case, his parents were willing to send their only child off to board in a distant town so that he could pursue academics rather than farming. This choice essentially guaranteed that he would one day leave the farm and never return. This action insured a larger future for Fr. Frahm, but it also spelled the death of the farm itself. His parents sacrificed the continuity of their life's efforts so that their son could become something more.

During the period Fr. Frahm was away, he lived in the home of a widowed Czechoslovakian woman, going home only on the weekends and holidays. He came to care for this woman deeply, and after her death was given a piece of her table china, which he kept for the rest of his life. He described her as a warm and caring person and he told me that she changed his world by accepting him for who he was. For four years he was allowed to be himself, largely free from the chaos of a violent family. I don't think it's an overstatement to say that without this respite, his life would have turned out very differently.

Like high school, college was an enriching experience. Fr. Frahm seemed to always thrive in an educational setting. He majored in psychology and philosophy and participated actively in music and drama. During this time, his interest in music brought him into contact with his future wife. It was also during this time that he became actively involved in religious activities, which moved him in a way that eventually lead to his confirmation as a member of the Episcopal Church.

I once asked Fr. Frahm about this period of his life, thinking that since he chose to go to Seminary, he would have fond memories of this period and the church he attended. But he spoke little about it and described it as a confusing time for him. He had no stories of conversion or a sense of calling. And in fact he seemed to minimize the entire event.

When I tried to understand the complete lack of investment in the events that led up to his chosen career I came to two conclusions. First, for Fr. Frahm, religion was a private thing. Your religion was yours and for it to have any meaning in your life at all you needed to keep it to yourself. Fr. Frahm believed strongly in the biblical idea that you needed to "work out your own salvation with fear and trembling."

Secondly, I think he had engaged in a bit of revisionist history. His difficulties with organized religion had to some degree caused him to reevaluate this period of his life and its meaning. He refused to clarify this question for me and the only clue he gave me about it came as the answer to a question I asked regarding my own interest in going to Seminary. I spoke about what I could learn and I expressed the hope that Seminary life would answer some of my questions about my self. He looked at me and said, "If you are thinking about attending Seminary, you should be considering what you could give to the church not the other way around."

In spite of all this, at some point during college the church became the primary focus in his life. By the time he reached graduation, he had expressed an interest in taking holy orders, something his academic record helped solidify. With the endorsement of the Dioceses of Iowa, he was offered a full scholarship to the Episcopal Theological Seminary in Cambridge, Massachusetts. His love of school and his motivation to stay away from home made it inevitable that he would snap up this offer and shortly after graduation, he was off to Boston.

Far away in Cambridge, Fr. Frahm told me he started to feel isolated and alone. He experienced frequent bouts of depression and anger. School and activities had always enabled him to manage and even suppress the after effects of his childhood but for some reason, it wasn't working any more. Fr. Frahm told me he wasn't happy during this period but never spoke in any detail about it. I assume however, that for some reason, he aged out of the ability to deny his feelings. Away from all he knew and unable to center himself, he started to suffered greatly.

At some point during this time period he began to drink. To what extent and with what frequency I am unsure, but it was a significant enough start to tear his life apart in years to come. This scenario is all too common. A person unable to manage or deny feelings will inevitably turn to something external that can do it. I would guess that probably better than 80 percent of alcoholics have a story that starts just like this. With little support and a tendency to keep his own counsel, he probably lost this battle as soon as it started.

Fr. Frahm talked often of enjoying the academic challenges of seminary. I have a collection of his research papers and it is clear that he loved to explore and contemplate the questions that were put to him. He maintained ongoing relationships with several of his professors for decades after he graduated. His friendship with Joe Fletcher a professor of philosophy, was something he treasured. He regularly spoke of the impact Professor Fletcher's course on situational ethics had on him. This impact was profound enough to last for Fr. Frahm's entire life.

He also spoke at length about meeting Paul Tillich when he was teaching his systematic theology at Harvard. Fr. Frahm told me about sitting in Tillich's lectures and how difficult Tillich could be for the students to understand. Tillich immigrated to the United States when Hitler came to power in Germany and had to learn English in later life. His accent was thick and Tillich had difficulty with many aspects of the language. When this occurred he would often mutter to himself in German which was impossible for most of the students to understand, except Fr. Frahm. Fr. Frahm could speak German before he could speak English. When he and Tillich discovered the linguistic connection to each other they were able to have many long conversations in German, which Fr. Frahm said changed his perceptions of what God could be.

Fr. Frahm loved to drop stories on me out of the sky. We would be feeding the birds and he would remark on how he knew or had spoken to some well known individual. One day after we had been reading T.S. Elliots' Ash Wednesday and were having a cookie, he reminisced about the afternoon when he met Elliot and the supper they shared. Apparently T.S. Elliot was visiting his sister in Cambridge and had come to Episcopal Service in the evening. Fr. Frahm met him on the way out and they struck up a conversation which lasted through supper and into the evening. Fr. Frahm told me the story about meeting Elliot but never spoke about their conversation. I assumed it must have been private.

Even in an environment like this, Fr. Frahm told me that if he had possessed the money he would have left on several occasions. Only his poverty kept him trapped at the Seminary. I don't know if the events are related but he said that several times during this period his depression and anger almost overwhelmed him. Apparently, everything was looking increasingly meaningless as time went on. He searched for a way to cope with this meaninglessness and found something important working with deaf children. Fr. Frahm, already fluent in three languages, now threw himself into learning American Sign Language and working with kids. The job stabilized him for a time, as service to others always seemed to do.

Each senior at Episcopal Theological Seminary was required to give a sermon to the student body which was evaluated by his peers and graded by the faculty. Fr. Frahm gave me a copy of that sermon, which begins "Exile – that is the theme for each of us. For to every man there is a kingdom, and from that very kingdom – an exile. It is the lot of each of us never to have his heart's desire, always to wander naked and alone." It is a snapshot of his internal world. He had discovered himself alone and knew that he was wondering, searching for something. I don't know for certain if he knew what it was he longed for, but as I look at his life I think he simply wanted to be loved. But, like most young people, he mistakenly thought that love had to come from outside him when, in reality, the only love that would help him would have to come from inside.

Nevertheless, he graduated from Episcopal Theological Seminary and was ordered to the diaconate of the Episcopal Church that same year. He married a former college classmate shortly after his return, and soon, was ordained to the priesthood and assigned to a parish in eastern Iowa. Somewhere during this period, he was involved in a car accident resulting in serious back injuries that caused ongoing physical problems and eventually led to his using a cane, and at times a wheel chair. These physical problems and the pain that they caused plagued him for the rest of his life.

I know very little about Fr. Frahm's history prior to my initial meeting with him. He spoke about himself but in reality he shared little. But Fr. Frahm never spoke about his wife and his marriage, at all. The details of his marriage, family, divorce, and subsequent family challenges were things, I believe, he kept very much to himself. From what little he told me and what I observed over time, it-is clear that his wife's departure and his divorce caused him to feel immense guilt and shame. This is one of those issues he had dealt with and accepted but it never went away. I think he kept the pain very close to his heart and used it as penance for his sins or as a reminder of what was real. Either way, I saw it almost every day.

What I did learn about this time of his life suggests that he was almost certainly battling alcoholism, and had been for some years. Alcohol use combined with his precise and exacting nature would not produce a happy home life. Knowing what I know about alcoholism and Fr. Frahm's personality I don't know if anyone could have stayed with him for very long. It would have been far too much to expect from anyone.

His alcohol use increased dramatically after his divorce. He was intoxicated every day and several people I spoke with made statements to the effect that it was amazing how much he could drink. He had reached a place where he had to be intoxicated or he would shake. Without alcohol in his system at all times he experienced symptoms of withdrawal. My discussions with those who knew him have convinced me that he was very close to death. What those around him told me he drank on a daily basis had to have taken him very close to alcohol poisoning. Between the risk of poisoning and the other health complications that accompany this level of drinking death wasn't an issue of how but when. I think he had ceased to care where he was going, and to some extent, was simply waiting for death to come.

There were a couple of people that entered his life at this point and their appearance seemed to slow his self destruction. He became very good friends with a professor of English at Wayne State College in Wayne, Nebraska. This woman was much older than he and they had between them a love for literature and poetry. She woke Fr. Frahm's love of poetry and got him started writing. She served as his teacher and editor for many years and her presence was everything to him.

They wrote poems, exchanged poems and talked poetry endlessly. She encouraged him to focus on his writing and even to give public readings of his work. She encouraged him to take a sabbatical of sorts and do some research and writing in England. Fr. Frahm loved England and you only had to hear him talk about it for a moment and you realized that this trip was one of the best things that had happened to him in some time. He spoke of it as if it was the beginning of his life and I think in many ways it was.

Although his drinking continued he had a new lease on life and he was in love with his new vocation as a poet. He was even taking steps to become more visible as a poet in the world. Soon after his return from England a friend introduced him to a woman who was to change the rest of his days. They dated and soon fell deeply in love with one another. Whereas some men would be satisfied saying I love you, Fr. Frahm gave her this poem found in Summer's Lease.

<u>This Love We Have</u>
Well, let it snow, and let the wind blow cold:
we sit together here before the fire,
its flames a sacrament of that desire

> which burns in me though I am growing old,
> and lovingly your slender arms enfold
> the me I gentled am, till I require
> nothing I do not have, and I aspire
> to naught but being held the way you hold.
>
> Unlike the sweetly scented apple wood
> by whose destruction is the house perfumed,
> which turns to ash as it gives forth its light;
> more like the bush before which Moses stood
> is this love we have, which burns on unconsumed,
> a cheering warmth against the winter night.

Jolene accepted him completely, exactly as he was. She returned his love, and in so doing, kept him hopeful, and I believe brought him back to life. She resurrected a part of him that was dead or might as well have been. She did for him what many others had been unable or unwilling to do—love him exactly as he was. And Jolene was able to not only love him as he was, but to love him when he felt he was at his worst. It was this love, and the help of other friends, that allowed Fr. Frahm to admit that he had a problem with alcohol. The love and strong commitment of these two would continue throughout the last 21 years of his life.

When Fr. Frahm emerged from treatment, he spent the next several years looking deeply into himself. It would seem that in the events leading up to his realization that he had a problem had awoken something inside him. He was compelled to spend much of his time in contemplation and silence. I don't know exactly what he found, but I think I have a pretty good idea. He attended a few AA meetings and although he believed in the AA process, he did not feel that it would work for him in the long term. He preferred to study, meditate, and volunteer his time counseling and hearing the "fifth step" of other alcoholics.

It was at this point that Fr. Frahm began to share his notion that you have to love yourself before you could be loved or love another. He saw this as a key to the problem of addiction and within the AA model he understood it to be of great importance. If you are going to turn you life over to a higher power and/ or make a fearless moral inventory of yourself you had better be able to love yourself first. Without love for yourself you could never turn anything over to God and the burden of a moral inventory would be too much to bear.

He gave a talk once to a group of addiction professionals and he told them, "Why what we think about ourselves should be important to the Creator of the Universe I don't know. But evidently it is and that's His or Her problem. It often offends us that God chooses to use what we believe to be our weaknesses to further His or Her purposes, but that's our problem."

He spent his first year after treatment, for the most part, alone in meditation or in study with the Rabbi at the local synagogue. For over two years, he did little but nurture whatever it was that had awoken inside him. He focused almost completely on his spiritual development and his place in organized religion. Over time, all organized religions seemed to interest him less and less. And slowly his experience of God developed into something that became the center of his life. The events of these years changed him radically into the person I would meet a decade latter.

Fr. Frahm was baptized initially in a small German speaking country church in Nebraska. But it was these initial post-treatment years that were his real baptism. One translation of baptism from the original Greek is "the immersion in sufferings." I'm sure this is an accurate description of what happened to him. It was an ordeal that would not have been suffered by many, but the process allowed him to find a way to love himself and this love grew in a way that changed him forever. He looked into his suffering and saw God staring back at him.

He may have seen God but he was still human and Fr. Frahm carried more than his share of pain, guilt, and shame into his adulthood. Particular pieces of his life seemed to constantly stalk him. He did not see these things as mistakes, character flaws, or personal weaknesses; he saw them as a process of becoming, and he often identified them as wolves. He talked at length about wolves in his childhood. He relayed stories of growing up on the plains of Nebraska, hearing the wolves howl at night while he lay in bed. He remembered winters when the wolves were so hungry they would come growling to the door of the house. Wolves figured largely in his spectrum of childhood fears. Today, children have the boogey man, but on the prairie of Nebraska in the 1930's even the boogey man was afraid of the wolves.

His adult life was a constant struggle with these wolves. The beauty of his life was in how he chose to struggle. He confronted his wolves, real or remembered, and he developed an interesting ability to tolerate their existence and ultimately to make friends with them. As he wrote in his poem "Wolf Song" in 2002:

> Again they come—and after all these years—
> who howled fell winds on many a childhood night;
> but now they raise adult, expected fears,
> since I roam meadows close to winter's white.
> Near the long snows the little plants grow sweet;
> here are the greenest grass, the brightest flowers.
> So why should not, to catch such easy meat,
> wolves from the past haunt all my present hours?
> Why should I be surprised to hears their cries
> rise louder still on ever colder airs?

> to see their shadows wait with patient eyes,
> or find the last breath heard not mine but theirs?
> I know it now, have sensed it all along:
> I go to feed one long high note of song.

Fr. Frahm knew that his wolves were coming for him and chose not to fight. He surrendered to them and allowed them to consume him and pick his bones clean. Even something as painful as this he did with love. As a result, there was much less violence toward himself and those around him—only a series of private moments that no one could witness, and then he was joined with his wolf forever. He accepted them as part of him and he of them. This practice enabled him to acknowledge his past, and to transcend it. He acknowledged the wolves honestly, for what they really were, and sat with them in acceptance and love. This practice made him whole and he became something larger.

I do not mean to suggest that he had complete control of his wolves all the time. Those who knew him well realized this was not the case. His wolves would appear on occasion in the form of anger and fear. He would act on these emotions and then realize what he had done. When he understood what had happened he took all the time necessary to greet his wolves and welcome them home. Very few people were ever privy to what was happening inside him. Short of the one woman he loved, I think only a handful ever heard him talk about it.

For 21 years, Fr. Frahm and Jolene were together and he had shown himself to her completely. She had accepted everything he had shown and loved him for who he was. She was the primary participant in his worst moments, as well as his best. She was able to accept these aspects of him no matter how angry or fearful they seemed, and he loved her because of this. I think he knew that without her love and acceptance at the beginning, nothing would have turned out the way it did. And no matter what he might have said to the contrary, she was precious to him.

He didn't speak a great deal about the times when he was overcome by what was inside him. When the wolves came and he reacted poorly, he took time to sit with what had just arrived. It was as if an old friend had stopped by to talk. The real appreciation I have for his ability to transcend his wolves was that he embraced them, not out of fear, but out of love, and inside this process emerged whatever he needed to feel peaceful and whole.

His ability to transcend suffering through love is precisely what he showed to others. It was the cornerstone of everything he taught. He constantly lived this transcendence and invited all of those around him to do it as well. In relationship with Fr. Frahm, a person could love him or herself, even the dark parts, and accept his or her mistakes, problems, and wounds with a loving acceptance rather than the usual fear, guilt, and shame. Here is a poem from Plains Songs that he wrote for someone who came to him.

<u>The New Old Bear</u>

These things I told you one cool autumn night:
no mere red measles' fever set to flight

that boy who lived in me till I was ten
and pushed him toward the race of silent men.

I mentioned how, when he began to mend,
he missed his Bear, his childhood's surest friend

whose shabby ears at least would hear and keep
secrets he sobbed before he fell asleep.

"Where is my Bear?" he asked, But no one knew.
They shoved the question off, as grown-ups do:

"Why would you want that dirty thing?" they said.
"It's old and full of germs. Now go to bed."

And lying in the dark alone, he learned:
because he'd gotten sick his friend was burned

along with truth and courtesy and such,
and boys and bears had never mattered much.

That night he lit a low slow fire of rage
and threw his boyhood in and came of age.

When, Bear forgotten forty years or more,
I shared what I had never told before,

I said it with a wise indulgent smile,
thinking he had not mattered all that while,

and only spoke intending to reveal
that childhood hurts—eventually—heal.

> Then Christmas came, after a month or two,
> bringing with it a new old bear from you.

> Oh, how could you have known, whom I call child,
> your gift would nearly drive an old man wild

> or guessed that I, who had not wept for years,
> could shed so many and such bitter tears?

Fr. Frahm's ability to transcend his wounds, combined with his efforts to live a life of love, gave hope to those who came to see him. He didn't just teach you, he lived the words he spoke. He was the words he spoke. He suffered, and he laughed. He was imprisoned but he was also free. He had won by surrendering completely. These contradictions were one of the secrets he tried to share with whoever would listen. He was as human as anyone who came to him, yet he was undeniably different as well. This made him appear larger than life to those around him.

There was a tendency in myself and I believe in others to "deify" Fr. Frahm. He was the first truly Holy thing I have ever known and his presence made the things around him Holy. When I looked at Fr. Frahm I could almost see God standing somewhere just over his shoulder. I won't speak for others but for me, Fr. Frahm was the yardstick by which I will forever measure all Holy things. Maybe there is a word besides deify that better fits this situation. If there is I'm not aware of it.

Many people deified Fr. Frahm right up until they heard he was dead. It was as if they believed he could mollify even Death himself. He would need only to sit down and tell him a story, read him a couple of poems, and Death would smile, finish his drink, and move on to the next house. I thought I had long since passed through the stage of deifying him, but I too, discovered that in his final days I thought he was more than human.

During the last three days he spoke less and less. When we had a quiet moment, I sat down on his bed and told him that I did not know how to handle what was happening. He had made me his power of attorney and told me what he wanted. I said I was hearing different things from different people and I was no longer sure of what I should do. I told him he would have to tell me what he needed from me. He took a long breath, smiled, and told me that he did not always know what he needed. As I looked at him lying there it came to me that I was relying on him to help me handle his death, rather than simply loving him and responding to him from moment to moment. I realized my mistake, kissed him, and spent the rest of that day at the foot of his bed, loving him and being there with him and for him as much as I could.

I watched others go through the same process. Most of the people who came to him needed something in their universe that would enable them to make sense out of nonsense and bring order out of chaos. Fr. Frahm could do this, and he wanted others to do it for themselves, but this takes time. Many of those who came to him did not have enough time. They knew it. Fr Frahm knew it as well, but nothing could be done about it. They said goodbye to him, or not, and walked out of his hospital room toward whatever was next in their lives. His love went with them.

The process of discovering who you are and then loving ALL of what you discovered can be, and I think often is, a lifetime project. If you were lucky, and you realized what you actually are, Fr. Frahm would offer you a deeper friendship. He offered a friendship beyond that of the teacher and student. It was a level of connection that allowed him to act more directly as a kind of "midwife" to your spiritual development. Those who were lucky enough to receive such friendship were truly blessed. I held this gift for only a short time and it changed every aspect of my life.

It was as a friend that I watched a deeply wounded man love a body and a memory riddled with pain. I saw him miss people who didn't come around very often. I watched his pain when those he had helped no longer needed him and moved on. Finally, I watched him come to terms with his diminishing health and make an active decision as to when and how he was going to die.

Many eastern spiritual traditions state that great teachers know when the time is right for them to die. Natural death is a long series of stages and choices to which a spiritual teacher is finely attuned and Fr. Frahm was no exception to this. He seemed to sense the end coming and decided to greet it with open arms long before it arrived. He spoke with no one about this, but had, for months, gone about the material and financial preparations for his end. Although he had given me hints about where he was going, I'm embarrassed to say I knew nothing until the evening he told me he was going to put himself in the hospital the next morning, and he wouldn't be coming out. I thought this was strange because, although he was ill, his condition didn't seem to warrant a statement like this. At 9 a.m. the next morning he walked into the hospital. Four days later he was gone.

# Part Two
# The Tool Box

Maybe you're already aware of a longing inside you and you're not really sure what to do with it. Or possibly you suspect that your life could become deeper and richer than it is right now. Whatever your situation, what follows is a tool box of sorts that will offer you a few ideas you can use to acquire a new perspective on things like freedom, love and reality. This next section is a step ladder to stand on and take a new and fresh look at the life you live. My hope is that you pick up one or two things that stick with you for awhile and ultimately teach you something new.

This is only an invitation. Some of the material will resonate with you. Some will not. All you need to do is consider what seems important or relevant to you. Take an idea, poem, or story and hold it. Sit with it in silence, and see what arises. Carry it around with you, and in your spare moments bring it out and look at it again. Do not bring an agenda or any expectations with you when you read, as this will only stifle your ability to learn. Just bring silence and see what happens. Just in case you are still concerned about what to do and how to do it, I will tell you a story.

Often when Fr. Frahm taught me, I did not understand the lesson. I would feel lost, confused and frustrated. At times I thought the whole endeavor, whatever it was, was kind of stupid. This didn't seem to bother him. He simply offered me an idea and watched to see what would happen. If it was a good day I would simply own up to my ignorance and say I didn't get "it," whatever "it" was. When this happened, Fr. Frahm would tell me this story from Anthony DeMello (1989).

Every month the disciple faithfully sent his master an account of his spiritual progress. In the first month he wrote, "I feel an expansion of consciousness and experience my oneness with the universe." The master glanced at the note and threw it away. The following month this is what he had to say: "I have finally discovered that the divine is present in all things." The master seemed disappointed. In his third letter the disciple enthusiastically explained, "The mystery of the One and the many has been revealed to my wondering gaze." The master yawned. His next letter said, "No one is born, no one lives, and no one dies for the self is not." The master threw his hands up in despair.

After that a month passed by, then two, then five; then a whole year. The master thought it was time to remind his disciple of his duty to keep him informed of his spiritual progress. The disciple wrote back, "Who cares?" When the master read those words, a look of satisfaction spread over his face. He said, "Thank God, at last he's got it!"

# Chapter Eight
# Fr. Frahm's Presence

The concept of presence is an idea that is not well understood. Everyone from TV talk show hosts to Buddhist monks have weighed in on the idea from one prospective or another. Even the most basic scan through popular media will quickly offer the guidance of someone suggesting, "You should breathe, find your center, and be present in the moment." As a culture we are inundated by books, magazines, therapy, yoga, meditation and Tai Chi all trying to teach us to be present in our day-to-day activities. Even after attending a three day workshop on how to be present most of us would be hard pressed to give a definition of what presence actually is...myself included.

With all this exposure to the practices of presence, how is it that we still fail to grasp what this idea means? The first reason, and one that I have mentioned before, is that once an idea reaches the popular culture it is frequently stripped of all its depth, tradition, complexity, and paradox in order to make it less threatening to our already established ideas, traditions, and preferences. American culture is legendary for the practice of skimming what we think is the cream from the top of some ancient wisdom and then presenting it as if we have everything of importance.

Once we have taken what works for us, the idea moves into the mainstream where it will be further victimized by sentiment and trivialities. In an environment of this sort, a truly important idea will have great difficulty surviving its adoption in a form that offers the depth of the original idea, whatever it may have been. The bottom line on this matter, and a point worth belaboring, is that our world rarely changes itself to accommodate new things. We tend to change things into something that we think will benefit us.

Even without our cultural practices and modifications, the concept of presence will still remain vague and difficult for the average person to understand. The primary reason for this however, is that like all spiritual ideas of any depth, you can't think your way to it. It can't be "understood" or "explained" by the mind/ego very well. The more you analyze, ponder, and critique it, the more it will escape you.

How in the world are we to grasp a concept like presence if everything from our culture to the functioning of our own mind works against it? The answer is that we can't really grasp it. Presence is a mystery. I can't explain what Fr. Frahm's presence was, why it benefited him or how he had such a profound impact on others. To attempt an explanation made up of ideas, like breathing, centering, stillness, and the present moment falls far short of the goal. All I can really say about Fr. Frahm's presence was that it was a mystery to me. And this mystery was everything.

Fr. Frahm never talked about presence, he was aware of the idea but believed it to be of little benefit to discuss. Many spiritual traditions believe that presence is the starting place for any practice or activity but Fr. Frahm didn't agree with this. "What good is an idea like presence if you have no idea what's actually happening inside you," he would say. He wasn't opposed to presence, but he clearly felt that most of us would get more benefit from being authentically who we are at this moment than from being present at this moment.

It was important to Fr. Frahm that you first worked with what was inside you. What you really thought and felt. You had to stumble through the difficulties and blind spots as exactly who and what you are at that time. Fr. Frahm was frequently concerned that attempts to be present were often attempts to avoid who you are and what you think and feel. He believed that you had to learn to love yourself and then to love others as exactly who and what you are, or any practice of presence would be hollow and often meaningless. I asked him once why he didn't teach more about presence and he remarked that "Learning to be present and not really knowing how to be you, is like being made captain of the Titanic."

Nevertheless he did have a thing or two to say on the matter. If someone came to him who was interested in "presence" as an idea or practice, he would give them what he could. He believed too much in the individual's path and the wisdom of following your intuition to do otherwise. But ultimately, he was always concerned that practices of presence were very frequently efforts to escape exactly what needed to be addressed.

Once you had a fair assessment of whom and what you were and you were honestly able to love yourself then Fr. Frahm was ready to talk about "presence". Of course he rarely called it presence, but simply recognized it as a kind of freedom. And if you were ready and interested, he would work with you regarding how you lived your daily life and how you could use every activity to cultivate love and freedom.

In the few times Fr. Frahm talked to me about presence he remarked that it would only come through serious, honest, and daily practice. He remarked that presence for him was not about "a moment" or a "center" it was about God. For Fr. Frahm presence was an effort to actually be present with God. It was the daily effort to let go of the boundaries that isolate us and with this you are closer to God. As I write this I can hear his voice saying "Don't desire presence, only desire God."

Presence is a paradox that can't be brought into being by the mind. Fr. Frahm taught that presence can exist only where the ego/self is not. Therefore, the more you intentionally and strategically think, the less presence you have. To achieve presence, according to Fr. Frahm, depended not on something you did, but on something you didn't do. It is not something you gained; it was more truthfully the absence of something. The something that needed to be absent was the mind, the strategic ego/self that holds us at its mercy most of the time.

Fr. Frahm taught me that being present may be a state of being but it was the doing that mattered. He said there were many methods, actions and activities which would quiet the mind (ego/self) and allow you to experience the stillness behind it. This stillness and the emptiness that follows were, for Fr. Frahm, the place he went to be present with God.

I realize that this short explanation makes presence seem far easier than it really is to achieve. But achieving presence isn't the point. For Fr. Frahm it was the attempt, the doing that was important because he knew that in the doing, you learned and changed. In the doing, if you were honest and diligent, you had to grapple with the illusions and boundaries that kept your ego/self in control and God at a distance. For Fr. Frahm, this was the heart of the matter.

The illusions your boundaries cast over your life originate in your mind. They are created by the mind out of a need for containment, security, and identity. In service of these illusions and the needs that arise from them, the ego will change, color and modify things to appear as it desires them to be. Fr. Frahm said repeatedly that it was within these illusions that human suffering is created and maintained.

You don't have to look far for an example of illusion at work. Your memory can give ample evidence of the phenomenon if you examine it closely. Many of us have become aware during the course of our lives that we have watched or participated in the same events with other people who have completely different memories of what happened. That person was right beside you, yet, remembers it differently. Thus, the same situation yields two interpretations, which are concrete examples of the mind/ego at work. It creates an experience that best fits its own perspective and best serves its needs. The mind/ego must always be first, it must always be the center of the universe. It is changing reality according to an agenda that guarantees its ongoing comfort and safety.

When you consider how much of this creating the ego does in a given day, it is fair to suggest that much of your history, and more significantly, your present is an illusion. It is highly probable, that you are experiencing a crafted present and past, and a fantasized future that serve the agenda of your mind/ego. You see almost nothing as it really is. Your day-to-day experience is one you are creating from the most self-centered place possible.

Presence should be considered both a verb and a noun. It is a being as well as a doing. In the ground of our daily lives it is a practice that you engage in to free yourself of the mind/ego and the illusions that it will always struggle to maintain. It is a practice of silence, or of loving, or of giving, or of serving, or of playing, or of just being, in which the mind becomes quieter and ultimately the ego/self falls by the wayside. What remains is consciousness as it truly is, not product of your individual mind, but the vibration of something larger, of which you are only a small part.

Fr. Frahm felt that without grappling with these illusions and boundaries, the journey for spiritual freedom is doomed before it starts. You have to work your way through these problems as you attempt to be present with God. This is the process of freedom. Everyone's process is different and almost anything can be used as a practice of presence. Fr. Frahm advised people to look around them and they would discover that many of the things they already do are about presence.

This is not as hard as it sounds. It's not esoteric or particularly difficult. Cultivating presence may be challenging, but the practice is not. In fact, it's quite easy. All that is required is an honest and diligent approach to any number of different paths. Fr. Frahm taught me that everyone has a sense of what it is to be closer to God. It happens to us every day, and in countless ways. Some people garden; others pray, sing, play, or love. Some dance, read poetry, walk, run, or serve other people. Still others just breathe and look out the window. Take a moment and think about your life. Is there something you do regularly in which the world and even your "self" starts to disappear?

It will be one of those ordinary activities in which every so often, more often if you're more advanced, the facts, worries, and planning of everyday life just melt away. This is not the same as dissociation or just zoning out for awhile. I'm talking about a moment, or longer, where the self you think you are fades into the background. No yesterday or tomorrow. No problems or joys. It's just existence, infinite and blissful.

Fr. Frahm would tell you to capitalize on what you already know. All you need to do is cultivate this practice and those like it, and your ability to achieve presence grows. Be loyal to your practice but always remember you are not learning something new, you are letting go of something old. Presence is not a desired product of activity it is the process itself. Practice brings about a change in the way you exist...right this moment. This change can occur anytime and anywhere; all you have to do is become more efficient at getting out of the way. "Be still and know that I am God", a wise man once said. There may be some who can't recall an experience of presence. Others may want to cultivate a different practice. For those people, I offer the following exercises (although I hate to call them exercises) I learned from Fr. Frahm.

**Exercise One:** Find a comfortable and quiet place to sit. Close your eyes and begin to breathe. Start by following your breath in and out. Try to feel the entire breath. What does the air feel like as it travels through the body and where exactly does it go? Each time you exhale, release and relax. The first impediment to a practice of presence is nervous tension. Whatever happens, whatever difficulties or struggles arise, just breathe and accept them with love. Accept the parts of you that will not relax and will not become comfortable. There is no struggle in presence, no wrong way to achieve it; just accept what is.

Simple as it sounds, this practice is not without difficulty. Your mind will race this way and that. It will distract you from the practice itself. Don't worry, just accept it. Return to your breath. You are not wrong, you have not failed, a distraction just is. Without any judgment you need only to return to your breath.

You will be uncomfortable and will fidget and need to adjust your body. Again, accept it with compassion. It is not wrong, it just is. Find comfort and return to your breath. Follow it in and out. On the exhale, release and relax, but always stay aware of the breath. If you lose your breath, simply return to it.

This practice will cultivate the acceptance and non-judgment that is needed to be present. You have to be able to accept what is happening without any self-judgment or emotional attachment. To do this in your practice will help you do it in your everyday life. To do it in your everyday life will help you do it in your practice. There is no difference.


**Exercise Two:** If you already have a practice or meditation in mind, whatever it is will be fine to use for this exercise. If you don't have a practice, just sit in a comfortable and quiet place. Breathe in and out a few times, relax, and find comfort. Once you are relatively quiet, find an object in your visual field or in you mind's eye and focus on it. This image can be a meaningful and symbolic one or something as common as the light switch. Don't worry, it makes no difference. Then, as you focus on the object, notice your mind. What does it do? For most of us it will run in all kinds of directions. Again, no judgment, just notice what it does. Then bring your mind home and focus on the object again. Your mind will run and run. I will venture a guess that as you do this exercise your mind will run off, and you will be carried away with it. Don't worry; whenever you catch yourself just return to your focus.

As you work with this practice you will find that your mind runs away less often. It will stay at home longer and become quieter over all. You will experience more stillness and peace inside. This stillness and peace will spill out of your practice and into your life. It will infect your days with peace, patience, and happiness. Hopefully, if you do the practice well, you can experience everything the same way you experience your practice. You will be still, empty, and so, truly present.

Presence is not something I can explain to you or help you to understand. If you desire presence or are just curious about it, all I can tell you is that you need to practice. As you work, you will find that presence is often an accident, but practice makes you accident-prone. Don't worry about presence...just practice.

# Chapter Nine
# A Spiritual Life

Human existence is surrounded by both wondrous beauty and great suffering. Because life changes every moment, there is no guarantee which of these will be next to visit you. The only certainty in this life is that you will experience both beauty and suffering, and you will frequently not understand why you see one and not the other.

The point here is that how we encounter beauty and suffering, how we understand them, is the key to the story of our lives. Most of us come to believe that our personal narrative is driven solely by our social, emotional, cognitive and biological elements. After all, what else is there? This notion is the prevailing wisdom of the day. And it is certainly not false; it's just not where the story stops.

Fr. Frahm felt that the social, emotional, cognitive and biological elements of life are certainly strong organizing forces but he felt that they only organize the more basic and ego driven aspects of who we are. Fr. Frahm saw these aspects of existence not as the sum total of the developmental spectrum but as the beginning. He felt that these elements constitute the most elementary of our developmental stages. He felt that behind and above this story, there was an all encompassing consciousness at work. And somewhere within each of us, the voice of this consciousness is longing. It is longing for a connection, a return to the larger consciousness from which it came. We long to experience our connection to God. Fr. Frahm felt that this longing is so important that it can, and should, be called the primary motive/drive in human existence.

The longing to connect with and experience God is the thing around which the self is constructed and organized. Even the ego/self/mind is organized around the sense of lack that our isolated existence causes. This lack is the sense that we are close to, but missing something that would provide safety, security, and wholeness. Beyond all the dogma and psychobabble lies a deep longing to connect with and experience the God that we sense we lack or have lost.

This longing for the larger divine consciousness beyond us is as much a part of the human being as it is an intuition. Each time we manage to move beyond our mind/ego for even a moment, we are confronted with the sense that there is a something real beyond our reality. When we fall in love, sit in nature, play with children, or meet good friends and we do it with honesty and love, we often feel this divine consciousness around us. Our existence expands. Suddenly we are not so much mind/ego (I am Bob, I am Jane) as we are connected to everything and everyone. In this moment, who you are (I am Bob, I am Jane) doesn't disappear, it just doesn't matter as much.

This expansion of existence also occurs when we encounter great suffering. In the midst of our pain, real or imagined, we can and often do disappear. The self fades into the background, and we are suddenly confronted with a larger pain, an abyss that threatens to swallow us whole. This phenomenon has been described as a black hole, depression, and the dark night of the soul. Whatever you call it, the feeling is the same. Those who have stood near the edge of this pain know it to be infinite and terrifying. This too is a connection with and experience of God, it is just another facet of him/her.

In these moments, when who we are expands and the mind/ego fades into the background, we can connect with this larger divine consciousness. We do not get larger; or actually "connect" to something. We simply find ourselves in the midst of something that has always been there. This encounter is a spiritual one and our sense of lack drives many of us to search for it, whether we are aware of the search or not. This search is the origin of most human beauty and suffering and, if done properly, the source of our ultimate liberation.

Fr. Frahm saw almost all human problems from this perspective. He saw them as spiritual problems. He knew that the primary drive in the human life is to achieve a union with God. Call it consciousness, spirit, soul, God, or whatever. He saw activities such as play, music, art, conflict, relationships, and even violence as attempts at, or opportunities for, an experience of God beyond the boundaries of the individual mind/ego.

Fr. Frahm felt that most of what people describe as problems are actually unsuccessful attempts to find and connect with God. He saw alcohol, drugs, food, relationships, cults (dare I say religion?), hobbies, inclinations, and patterns of behavior as attempts to find the larger divine consciousness (God) beyond the mind/ego. All of these problems are the result of the compromise made between the original longing/sense of lack and the mind/ego's need to be secure in its own reality.

The problem is that these actions and so many others are not the doorway that bring you to God. They cannot offer any real transcendence because the ego-self can never allow this. The human ego/self seems to know intuitively that to transcend it's self, it must do away with it's self. Because of this double bind, the ego will not easily offer you a sense of connection to anything other than itself. All the activity and behavior you engage in will promise an experience it cannot deliver. Your ego tells you that if you drink this, go here, use this, do this, worship here, or join this you will find what you are looking for. In the short term you will feel good but the experience, because it is an illusion, because it can end nowhere but at the ego-self, will result in disappointment and frustration.

From Fr. Frahm's perspective the problem was not a problem. When it was approached correctly the problem was an opportunity to find what you were looking for. But this opportunity, like most, is fraught with danger. You may begin to identify your relationship with the problem as who you are, and in doing so; you will miss the chance to move beyond it. Once you identify the problem (unhappiness, grief, shame, guilt, failure, depression, anger) as part of who you are, or worse, what you are, that is where you stay.

The mechanism that tries to save you is the fact that all problems have symptoms. A "symptom" is a voice from within stating that something inside you is not satisfied and longs to find what is real. Fr. Frahm's focus, therefore, was to listen closely to this voice and clarify what it says. He would, with creativity and fierceness, sit with you and invite you to listen to this voice, not with fear but with love and curiosity. Out of this experience would emerge productive and useful guidance.


**Exercise One:** One of Fr. Frahms' favorite activities was to sit with a question. Sitting with a question requires you to hear it and then just sit with it. Don't go looking for an answer to it, just hold it in silence and see what emerges. Try this for yourself. Pick an aspect of your life that troubles you. Take whatever it is and condense it to a word or a few words. At most, condense it to a short sentence. Remember, words tend to hide things. Let's call what troubles you X.

Now sit, and try to be comfortable. Try, as much as you can right now to be silent. Take as much time as you need to cultivate this. When you are ready, say to yourself, "What is it within me, that is good, that is troubled by X?" Many people want to say, "Why do I do X?" This allows them to repeat to themselves all their flaws and failures. If you take this route the answers you are giving yourself are just more of the same problem. Self condemnation will rarely reveal anything of value. Fr. Frahm always told me that "Only a genuine, decent, and reasonably good soul is troubled by your X." That is who/what you are looking for.

Ask your question and hold it. See what arises. No matter what comes, you should accept it with love. This step is absolutely necessary but it is not easy. There is a strong pull within us to focus on what we have done wrong. Self condemnation is seductive. It allows the ego/self to feel special and unique. Your problem becomes the only thing in the world and the worse pain anyone could experience. The ego/self becomes the new center of the world. Only by loving what is good within you that is troubled by your X, will you be able to see X for what it really is and then follow it to whatever is next.

Whatever you experience (thought, memory, feeling, perception), if you allow it to exist, it will take you to another experience. All experience is organized and will flow in a sequence that follows a natural logic. I cannot give you any answers except to tell you to sit and follow the experience you have. Remember to breathe and then, with love, slowly entertain one thing at a time. Don't worry so much about being correct, just be honest with yourself and everything will be fine. An honest response to what arrives will take you on a journey. The trip, if done well, will be worth your time.

Fr. Frahm never gave anyone a set spiritual path to follow nor did he give many specific directions regarding which path was better or best. He believed and he taught that God presents himself in countless ways. Given the fact that each individual is unique and will need to meet God on a very unique set of terms, seeing one perspective or some simple set of guidelines as correct is pointless and often dangerous. Fr. Frahm would suggest to you that all you need to do to live a spiritual life is to get really tired of your "self." You only need to stop telling yourself all the things you have told yourself to feel okay and embrace an empty, silent, vulnerability.

All true spiritual paths must originate in a place of not knowing. The more you know, the more your mind/ego assumes control, and the less you can experience and learn. You probably don't have to think very long to recall someone in your life who is willing to give spiritual advice but seems to live a life that is not terribly spiritual. I think we have reason to be concerned that those who give us spiritual advice today have little basis in experience from which to give it. Our spiritual advisors are often people who chose to go into a religious field or felt a calling to do so rather than a person who is honestly awake and alive.

For you and I most of our spiritual development took place under the auspices of a church. This is not a particularly bad thing, but at ground level it means that your spiritual life has been measured by sacrament and participation rather than on the basis of direct experience and real learning. Religious dogma surrounds us with teachings and rituals that are culturally, and in some instances such as marriage, legally binding even if the parties involved have no spiritual understanding at all. It is also possible to be saved by religious dogma, ritual, and sacrament without even the slightest understanding of it or yourself. In this scenario, your spiritual path is based on a legalistic relationship rather than on the discovery of who and what you are. St. Clement might have been thinking of this problem when he said "He who knows himself knows God."

A spiritual path is one of doing and being. No one can give this to you. You alone must sit in silence and learn to quiet your mind. When the self becomes still, you can put your mind/ego aside. Then you can experience God and realize that he has been part of you and apart from you since the beginning. Only here will you find the peace and wisdom that will allow you to sit with the beauty and suffering of this life and not find yourself mired in illusion. Only through direct experience of the divine, will you develop real spirituality.

Fr. Frahm's personal spirituality was based on his understanding of emptiness. He believed that a spiritual path was a movement toward God in which you were able to experience God's presence in this moment. Experience was the whole point. He did not want an intellectual or theological explanation for this experience. He did not want to have faith that God was real. He wanted to feel it and to love it right now. He thought it unnecessary to wait until you passed on to some after-life to be with God. The emphasis of all his teachings suggested that God was available right now. All you have to do is move toward emptiness.

Emptiness, as Fr. Frahm presented it, was not some void or transcendental nothingness. Emptiness was a place of silence and beauty in which the "self" was not present. You become empty when your everyday "self," this thing you have come to recognize as you, is no longer in the driver's seat. In emptiness, your "self" or "ego" or "identity" has been shed, as a snake would shed its dead skin, and put aside for awhile. The "you" you thought yourself to be is no longer first, and in that silent emptiness you can experience God.

Sometimes our experience of this emptiness is profound, such as the birth of a child or an experience of nature that leaves us completely empty for a short time. Other experiences of emptiness occur on a daily basis, though at a much less profound level. Examples of this include looking in the eyes of a loved one or engaging in your favorite activity until you lose the surface levels of your "self."

Fr. Frahm taught that the experience of emptiness could be developed and cultivated until it became a normal part of daily life as opposed to an extraordinary event in our lives. With emptiness as an aspect of daily living your experience of God is available to you all the time, no matter what is happening around you. There is nothing but God.

So what exactly does it mean to find emptiness, and how do we do this? Well, that's a tricky question. And by tricky, I mean that no other person can tell you exactly how to find it and you should beware of those who tell you they can. You will never find emptiness in language. Language is a product of, and a tool of, the mind/ego. Most of the time, when you speak, you speak from the "self." Therefore, words are not very useful in teaching or understanding emptiness. But they can be used to point the way. Fr. Frahm used words to point at the possibility of emptiness and to point at paths you might take to explore it.

**Exercise Two:** Emptiness, presence, and all other non-dual concepts can't be proven in logical argument. But you can get a feel for it as an experiential fact. As you read this, you see the words, the white page, and probably a few objects in the periphery of your sight. Take a moment and notice what you see in detail. Now, try to find the seer. As you are seeing, go into yourself and attempt to locate who or what is doing the seeing. Take quite some time to do this. You will find that no matter where or how you look, the seer is impossible to find. You will only find what you see. What you see is your experience of the seer. The same results will occur if you go looking for the hearer or the thinker. You will find only what you hear and what you think. This experience can, in the right environment, lead you to the inescapable conclusion that there is no separate self apart from the world. There is no gap between you and what you experience (see, hear, think, feel, etc.). "You" do not exist. "You" are a creation of the mind. If you are struggling with that idea, Fr. Frahm would smile and say, "Good, keep it up."

As the self falls away, what remains is rich emptiness. With no "self" to serve as a boundary between you and the universe, you can enter into relationship with the larger divine consciousness at the center of all life. This divine consciousness is not the God we have created in our image, but a God of eternal love that flows around and through everything in the cosmos including you.

So, where is a good starting point if you wish to have a taste of this emptiness? I will give you what I think Fr. Frahm would have given you if you had asked him what was so important about emptiness. Remember, he would only point to the truth, not hand it to you. First, he might have read this verse:

> Have this mind among yourselves, which you have in Christ Jesus,
> who, though he was in the form of God, did not count equally with
> God a thing to be grasped, but **emptied** himself, taking the form of
> a servant, being born in the likeness of men.
>
> Philippians 2: 5-7, RSV

He would have looked at you to see what sense you made of what he had offered. He would watch you closely because he never give you more than you needed. He would ask you to think about it for awhile. If he did not see signs of understanding in you, he would probably have read you this poem from Lao Tzu:

> <u>San-shih fu</u>
> We join spokes together in a wheel,
> But it is the center hole
> That makes the wagon move.
> We shape clay into a pot,
> But it is the emptiness inside
> That holds whatever we want.
> We hammer wood for a house,
> But it is the inner space
> That makes it livable.
> We work with being,
> But non-being is what we use.
>
> *(Mitchell, 1991)*

After reading this, he would smile and leave you to ponder what he had said. If you were ready, and your longing was strong enough, you would come back to him with more questions.

Fr. Frahm's spirituality was uniquely his. He saw it as one way, not the only way, to connect with God. He did not want a relationship with God. He wanted to submit to, be consumed by, and become one with God. He was not interested in religious faith or any system of beliefs. God was a reality that lived within him and within everything and everyone else. All one needed to do was to move toward emptiness. He often said, "Only when the self is gone will God be perceived." This is one of those "only(s)" that may take a lifetime.

## Stories

What follows are stories relevant to spirituality and the spiritual path. Some make specific points. Some pose more questions. Hold the story and see what arises for you. Read them in a quiet place. Carry them into your world. If they offer you something right away, great; if not, just hold onto them, and they're likely to show up at some point in the future.

Jesus tells a parable about the Shepherd with 100 sheep. One sheep wanders off, and the Shepherd is so concerned that he leaves the 99 to find the one. Once he finds his lost sheep, he brings it back to the flock. This is, of course, a wonderful story of parental love and devotion, but I always thought it was important that after he found his sheep and brought it back to the flock, the story never mentions that he did anything to mend the hole in the fence.

......................................................

An older woman came to see Fr. Frahm to ask his advice. He had been a priest in the dioceses for over 20 years, and she was troubled by a direction her parish was taking. She told him her story about her congregation pressuring the members to raise funds for an addition to the church. He gave her his thoughts. She thanked him and left. As he watched her pull out of the driveway, he said to nobody in particular, "Wouldn't it be nice if people could have a legitimate spirituality that others couldn't use to make money?" Then he turned to me and said, "In spite of what anyone has ever told you, God doesn't require financing. Anyone who suggests otherwise should separate his or her needs from God's."

......................................................

One day, Fr. Frahm and I were discussing people's behavior. I said that I felt it didn't matter what I did as long as I didn't hurt anyone else. He looked at me, smiled, and told me this story.

In the Talmudic tradition there are two separate punishments set out for the burglar and the robber. Of the two crimes it is the burglar who is punished more severely. He was quiet for a moment, looked at me, and asked me why this was. I told him I didn't know. He said that the robber commits his crime where God, you, and anyone else can see. The burglar commits his crime where only God can see. Therefore the burglar must care more about what men say and think about him than what God says and thinks about him. For that reason, he is punished more severely.

................................................................

It was a warm August afternoon and I started to talk about a person who I felt had wronged me. I said I was having trouble letting this go. I was, in fact, considering an act of retaliation. Fr. Frahm told me that, indeed, I was entitled to my feelings. Then he leaned back in his chair and got a very serious look on his face.

"It seems to me that God cares very little about what other people think about us or even what He thinks about us. But if He is a God worth his salt, He will care very deeply about what we think about ourselves. Judaism teaches that if a man comes to steal your coat you give it to him freely. Then you offer him your shirt as well. Do you know why this is?" He said. "No," I answered. "When you give your coat freely, you keep him from becoming a thief. When you offer your shirt, you not only keep him from being a thief but you make him someone worthy of a gift."

................................................................

I have always felt fascinated by the relationship between Moses and God. I have, over the years, read and studied the interactions between the two, particularly the ideas about the conversations on Mount Sinai. One day, I asked Fr. Frahm, "Why was it important to God that Moses should remove his shoes as he stood on holy ground?"

He listened to my question and announced quite casually that he had an idea or two about this. He said that at many holy places you must remove your shoes before you go in. This is done out of respect but also to remind you that to find God all you need to do is to take off everything that covers your soul. Taking off your shoes is symbolic of taking off the self that stands between you and God. I then asked him why God felt he had to tell Moses that he was on holy ground. He answered, "So that hopefully Moses would look down and realize that he had been standing on holy ground his whole life and if he could do that, he would learn that all ground is holy." Then he looked at me mischievously and said, "It is no accident that the bottom of a bare foot is called the sole (soul)."

................................................................

Jesus went to a hilltop to pray. He said, "Lord I am trying to teach them about themselves but it is difficult for them to hear me. They only want to worship me." God said, "I know, my son that has been a problem for me as well." Jesus said, "I have tried to tell them stories about themselves, but it seems to only confuse them." The Father said, "You're probably right. You had better tell them one story over and over again and hope that over time they will hear." Jesus said, "Won't they get bored?" God answered, "I have been telling them the same thing for years. I am always amazed by the fact that they hear something different each time."

Here is another of Fr. Frahm's poems from Plains Songs.

### I, John, Alone: On Reading the Nicomachean Ethics

"For one swallow does not make a summer, nor does one day; and so too one day, or a short time, does not make a man blessed and happy."

–Aristotle, Nicomachean Ethics, I, 7

Two swallows made a summer
one August afternoon.
Three meadowlarks in concert
improvised a tune
that set the grasses whispering,
which woke one cricket up.
Then he, on bent arthritic knee,
quite overfilled my cup.
By urgent stridulations
he bade me lift my eyes
to see a high hawk compassing
circles of Sandhills skies.
I raised the ethereal chalice
to toast the wheeling bird,
when such a silence interposed
as I have seldom heard.

For wine-sweet air caught sunlight
and, bending its trenchant rays,
so prismed earth's tired colors
that I grew drunk on praise.
Never, since dawns on Eden,
had bluestem shone so green;

nor, since Croesus' coffers,
had such bright gold been seen
as glowed where drying thistles
bowed before rising wind.
Herb scent, lent by sagebrush,
lulled a besotted mind
that reeled bewildered, enamored
 of motion, of shape and hue.
And not, since the world's creation,
such crystalline welkinblue.

Away in a Sandhills hollow
back of the back of beyond,
a glistening, shimmering beryl—
three acres of reed-fringed pond—
lay like a quiet gospel
opened to peace and rest.
There, like the gentle Luke, a swan
had built her halcyon nest.
Albeit that summer was largely gone,
she kept her bed of soft white down,
guarding her shrine of nativity,
her full-fledged cygnetry.

There, too, for wondering delight,
a great blue Matthew heron,
called from a day's receipt
of grudging minnow custom,
stood stranded in gray decision
as if on high behest;
as if in him the equipoise
of silence coalesced.

At last a Marcan redwing
summarized the scene;
his on brief skirl of tragic
epitomized serene.

I, John, alone in exile,
aging and gazing west,
am come away word layden
to limn a land of the blest.

For, once, three larks and a cricket,
two swallows, one blackbird and I
distilled a holy silence
and sang to sacred sky.

*So, excuse me, Aristotle,*
*but you perhaps have erred:*
*sufficient summer can indeed*
*be made by one small bird.*

*One day may make a season,*
*at least for such as we-*
*apostles of that reason*
*called infinity.*

If you sit quietly, you will hear the voice of God.

One of my many habits that I think Fr. Frahm found entertaining is my tendency to always lean toward intellectual reasoning rather than experience in my learning process. I spent a lot of time questioning him on what I should read or study rather than what I should be doing. Once I pressed him regarding reading material. He turned to me and said, "I believe that the Holy One authored a creation before He wrote a book, or caused one to be written, and His signature can be discerned on the former and questionably on the latter. If you want to know about God, all you need to do is spend more time being and less time reading."

Then he told me this story.

A student asked his teacher, "How can I find God?"

The master responded, "The harder you look, the more distance you create between Him and you."

The student said, "What can I do about the distance?"

The master replied, "Understand that the distance isn't there."

The student was confused and asked, "Does than mean the God and I are one?"

The master smiled and said, "Not one. Not two."

The student shook his head and said, "That is not possible."

The master stated, "The sun and its light, the ocean and its waves, the singer and the song—not one. Not two."

One afternoon, Fr. Frahm found me reading several theology books, bouncing back and forth between them, taking notes and then double checking my information with the Bible. He stood behind me for some time as I finished what I was writing. When I looked up he said, "When you make love to your wife do you use a book to tell you when, where, and how to do it?" I smiled at him, knowing this was going to go somewhere interesting, and said, "No." "Do you think she would tolerate you for long if you did?" "Probably not," I said. As he walked away he said, "And neither will He."


I thought this would be a good ending for this section. At the time I found the lost story both important and amusing. As time passes, I find it less amusing and more important. Books (no matter what book), methods, scholarship, reason, faith cannot replace a basic simple love. Nothing else matters. Nothing else could possibly matter.

# Chapter Ten
# Christianity and Faith

Fr. Frahm didn't have much time for the idea of faith. He considered it to be a bane on most people, and on Christians, in particular. He felt that our cultural and individual focus on faith made it difficult for us to seriously entertain the idea that we could know and experience God today. He often said to me, "Your time would be better spent if you focused not on faith in tomorrow but on living with God right now." His point, of course, was that if you work to cultivate an experience of God today, faith in a dogma or an afterlife becomes unnecessary.

Some people need faith. Fr. Frahm went to great pains to tell these people that there was nothing wrong with having faith, but ultimately it occurred only in their minds. It is largely an intellectual choice that we make, a belief we chose to adopt, concerning things we have no experience of. Fr. Frahm knew that because faith is a product of the mind, it will never be able to give you an experience of God right now. And this, of course, was what he wanted for everyone.

For faith to be of any use, Fr. Frahm thought it should be understood as an ongoing and unfolding experience of your relationship with God. Like all relationships, your experience will grow and change over time. It will have good days and bad. Some days, your experiences will leave you with less "faith", whereas other days will reaffirm everything you hoped for. Faith should be the after effects of an unfolding experience, not a choice made in the absence of experience. Therefore, "faith" must be a life-long process, a becoming, and we have no business flogging ourselves (or anyone else) because we or they lack it at some particular moment.

For Fr. Frahm, faith just wasn't a useful idea. He focused instead on a simple trust that grew out of his experience with the One at the center of everything. Faith pertains to something you can't see, feel, or hear. Trust, on the other hand, can and does emerge in a relationship between two parties, both of whom are actually here. This relationship, like all relationships, has to be tended to daily. You can attend to it in everything you do, from making breakfast, to interacting with co-workers, to putting your children to bed. All this, if done with love, can be about your experience of the divine.

Remember when I said earlier that Fr. Frahm treated those who came to see him as if they were God in disguise? This is why. For Fr. Frahm, God was everywhere and in everyone. When you came to see him, he saw God inside you. Everything he did and everyone he spoke to was part of his experience of God. I'll admit this idea is a bit abstract even to me. Nevertheless, this was Fr. Frahm's reality.

If you can see everything around you as God, and of God, then everything you do is with God and for God. Every moment of every day is an opportunity, in all its chaos and wonder, to cultivate an actual experience of God that is not faith-based nor does it exist solely between your left ear and your right. This type of interaction builds a trust based on your experience of the divine, not your idea of, or faith in the divine.

For this reason, Fr. Frahm encouraged rebellion, doubt, anger, distrust, and any other legitimate human response to God, and suggested that it is all part of your developing experience of whatever God is. The prerequisite for a successful experience of this kind is, of course, honesty with your self and authenticity in your life. If you intend to reach God without being honest with yourself and fol-lowing your own intuition, then your "experience" will only be in your mind.

Fr. Frahm often remarked that his experience was a running love affair with God that included spats. He would say, "God does not need my faith to feel good about who he is or to feel good about who I am." This notion is liberating because it means that you don't need to have faith in anything. You only need to trust in your own unique path to God. No matter how troubled, useless, or painful it might seem, Fr. Frahm would encourage you to believe that your path has value, and if followed with seriousness and honesty, will take you to a destination worth going to. If doubt is your path, follow it. If it is anger or love, you do the same. You need to nurture your own way, regardless of other people's perceptions. I have to stress, however, that it is necessary to be honest with yourself and avoid judgment while you follow any path or the process will go nowhere. You will be trapped within yourself, damaged, damage others, and your journey will not be a good one.

Fr. Frahm's path started as one of doubt and anger. It became one of love. He needed no faith. In fact he needed no answers at all. He had caught a glimpse of God, and he spent the rest of his days loving him. It was so simple. Just love him and everything else will take care of itself. All ideas beyond this come from man, not God.

**Exercise One:** Since I do not work to develop faith, I have no exercises to share. What I believe to be beneficial is the trust that grows out of a daily expe-rience of God. This exercise, then, will serve as an extension of the work you have probably already done. Whatever your favorite contemplative or meditative practice or daily activity, you can use it as the basis for this exercise.

Do your activity for awhile until you settle into it. Then take a moment to ask yourself what you would like to express to God right now. Make sure you can boil it down to a word or a very short sentence. It should be simple. Then return to your activity, and find your settle into it again. When you are ready, you should express yourself to God through your body, movement or breath. Do not think it or say it. You should express and display yourself in a spontaneous fashion. Don't worry about it and don't censor it. Just follow your heart at that moment. After some time of doing this, take a break and just settle into your activity again. Pause and experience the results of this practice.

**Stories**

Here are a few stories relevant to faith and its different aspects. I invite you to read and consider them. Feel free to take whatever they offer and walk away from the rest. Don't worry if you are right or wrong. It doesn't matter. Take your time, breathe, and be present.

I was listening to Fr. Frahm talk to someone who was going through a divorce. Fr. Frahm himself had gone through this process not 20 years earlier. He listened to the woman as she spoke about how she was handling her feelings. She said she wanted to purchase new clothes and furniture in order to start over again. He looked at her and said, "Ah, yes, when our souls are empty we fill our lives with things." She began to cry. I think the point Fr. Frahm was making is that the only thing that will fill the soul is God.

Fr. Frahm loved to tell a story about St. Teresa of Avila, whom he deeply admired. St. Teresa was riding her mule from one town to another when the mule bucked, and she fell into the mud below. As she got up from the ground she looked into the sky and said, "God, it's a wonder you have any friends if this is the way you treat the ones you have."

For Fr. Frahm this was not just a story; it was a suggestion about how one could be in a living relationship with God. Fr. Frahm told this story with the intensity of someone plotting a treasonous act. He wanted you to forget everything you had been taught, so you could come to God in a way that made sense to you.

In the book of Genesis the serpent is called the father of lies when, in fact, he told the complete truth. Eve told the serpent that God said if they ate the fruit they would surely die. That was the moment where the father of lies told the whole truth: Ye shall not surely die. But he told the truth with the intent to deceive, because he knew that what man will always fear above all is physical death. The reason God told Adam and Eve not to eat the fruit is that he knew if they did they would suffer a spiritual death

One day, when we where talking about faith, I said, "With you shooting down everything I have ever thought about faith, how am I supposed to have any?" Fr. Frahm said, "How do you expect to fly if you can't leave the nest of your own beliefs? As long as you cling to your ideas, you will never fly but you'll be very busy flapping your wings."

When I first met Fr. Frahm, I asked him endless questions about the nature of God. One day he turned to me and said, "God begins and ends in mystery. He is the unknowable. Every statement made about him by me or anyone else would be like pointing to his shadow." I thought about this for awhile and said, "Then how can we talk about God at all?" He took me to his garden pointed to some birds at the feeder and said, "Let's listen to them sing."

"To what can I compare this generation? They are like children sitting in the marketplaces and calling out to others: 'We played the flute for you, and you did not dance; we mourned and you did not weep.' For John came neither eating nor drinking and they say, 'He has a demon.' I came eating and drinking and they say, 'here is a glutton and a drunkard, a friend of tax collectors and sinners.'"

Matthew 11: 16-19; cf. Luke 7: 31-34

Christianity was something Fr. Frahm had largely given up on. He had rejected many of the dogmas of his church. He rejected anything that was not alive and honest. The one piece of Christianity that he embraced was the life of the man Jesus. He saw in the life of this man something extraordinary, but he saw it in his humanity, as well as his divinity.

Jesus was an individual, and he lived his life in freedom, without boundaries. He made his own relationship with God. He defined himself. He lived and acted according to what he felt to be correct, and he accepted those around him for who they were. He acknowledged that John the Baptist had one approach to the spiritual world, and he had another. Jesus makes no judgment as to who or what is best, but in the passage from Mathew cited above he seems to suggest that the real issue is something else.

Jesus did not rebel against Judaism or advocate some position called Christianity. He lived and taught the understanding he had of man and his relationship to God. "Love the lord your God with all your heart and with all your soul and with all your mind. This is the first and greatest commandment. And the second is like it: Love your neighbor as yourself. All the Law and the Prophets hang on these two commandments" (Matthew 22: 37-40).

Jesus knew that when others pipe you don't have to dance, and when they mourn, you need not weep. But he also knew we would pay a price for this freedom. Jesus had to have known what all free people eventually learn. Freedom catalyzes hostility. As a free being, Jesus revealed the lack of freedom in those around him. John Paul Sartre said, that to be subjected to the freedom of another is humiliating. Jesus embodied extraordinary freedom and it is quite likely that those around him found this humiliating. History has shown us through the lives of Jesus, Ghandi, Bonnhoffer, King, and so many others that if you insist on living in freedom, forces will coalesce and work to control or destroy you. "From the days of John the Baptist until now the Kingdom of God has suffered violence, and men of violence take it by force." (Matthew 11: 12)

Every day, Jesus risked paying the price of living in freedom and inviting others to do the same. In his world, he knew where his work would take him, and those around him had to know it as well. Yet, in the face of all this, he continued to teach that if you live in freedom you can have a deeply spiritual life.

Fr. Frahm understood Jesus' importance to human history and human life as arising not out of his divinity but out of his everyday living. His model for us arose less from what he said, than how he lived. He had a difficult childhood in which it is very likely that those around him considered him a bastard. It is evident that as he grew, he had problems with his family, and as an adult he was persecuted and ultimately killed. Yet in all things and at all times, he lived and taught in freedom.

That he was all divine or half divine or just human makes no difference. Like all human beings, he was afraid, and he prayed for the possibility that he might not have to pay the price for how he lived. But when the time came, he died authentically and completely free. It is precisely because Jesus lived as a human being that his life and death achieved such importance. One could expect great things of the son of God, but when a human being lives and dies this way it becomes a miracle.

............................................................

Once, having been asked by the Pharisees when the kingdom of God would come, Jesus replied, "The kingdom of God will not come with careful observation, nor will people say 'Here it is' or 'There it is,' because the kingdom of God is within you." (Luke 17:20-21) Thomas Merton said, "My experience tells me that the Kingdom of God is within us, and that we can realize it not by saying, "Lord, Lord," but by doing His will and His work. If, therefore, we wait for the Kingdom to come as something coming from outside, we shall be sadly mistaken.

(Quoted by Ghandi, 1964, 37:261)

As the Maharishi Ramana has said, "the ordinary Christian won't be satisfied unless he is told that God is somewhere in the far off heavens, not to be reached by us unaided; that Christ alone knew Him and Christ alone can guide us; that we must therefore worship Christ and be saved. If he is told the simple truth that "the kingdom of heaven is within you," he is not satisfied, and will read complex and far fetched meanings into it. Only mature minds can grasp the simple truth in all its nakedness."

Jesus repeatedly made the assertion that God and the kingdom of God are available to all human beings all the time. He went out of his way to point out that this kingdom, the place in which God manifests him or her self, is within us. Jesus' life implies that the only place God could ever make his or her presence known is within and among human beings. He taught that God was not in the churches, synagogues, governments, movements, groups, or political parties but inside every human heart every moment of every day, and he is here right now.

As I said a moment ago, the lesson of Jesus' life, according to Fr. Frahm, was not in what he said but in how he lived his life and ultimately died. The life of Jesus is a lesson for us on how to live our lives each day. If you can live your life as Jesus did, all that business about redemption and forgiveness will take care of itself. It is the way he lived that is his legacy to human beings. His humanity and behavior in the face of pain, rejection, accusation, betrayal, judgment, and finally death suggests to us that one can live in freedom with God every day no matter what happens around us. Jesus lived as a free man, free of the judgment of self as well as the judgment of others. He was free to love in a way that most of us can scarcely realize, and that is what made him divine. When the world persecuted him for living in freedom, he did not resist. He did not hate. He did not judge. He loved. This was the lesson of his life, and he offered it to each of us to be practiced every day. We can, indeed, live our lives as he did. Not as Christians, not as religious people, not as Americans, not as Republicans or Democrats, but as just you and I.

**Exercise Two:** There is a practice common to Hinduism I have found to be of immeasurable spiritual benefit. It is translated as "remembrance of the name." It is often called mantra, but this word sells the practice short and does little to convey its usefulness and power. The process is simply that of repeating the name of God.

This practice of repeating God's name has been advocated by many saints and mystics of the Greek and other Orthodox churches and it is a foundation of Buddhism and Hinduism. Mahatma Gandhi believed this practice was all that was necessary in daily prayer. It is said in the countries and cultures of Asia that if you repeat the name of God with all your heart your life will be transformed.

I suggest most often to those I work with, that they find a name for God that rings true for them. Since God is everywhere and in everything, the result will be the same regardless of the word(s) you use. Some people choose the word 'Jesus," others "Father," and some, "Lord." Again, it makes no difference. Find a quiet place, close your eyes, and breathe until you feel calm. See in your mind a thing or place you associate with your God. Then hold this picture in your mind and say the name on each breath. Don't worry about how or when. Just be present and say His name with love and devotion. If you tire, rest for a moment. Return to the practice when you are ready. Sit with this as long as it is comfortable; it is better to do three minutes of devotion than twenty minutes of distraction. Don't worry about the details. If you do this each day with love and devotion, your life will change itself. Your devotion will grow and your understanding of your relationship to God will deepen.

## More Stories

A man had led a life of sin and wished to repent. His sins were great and he felt he needed to go to the greatest saint in the land. When he arrived at the ashram of this saint, the man was out visiting others. One of the disciples of the great saint took pity on the man and instructed him to go into the yard and sit. When he felt ready, he should say the name of God ten times. The disciple told him that if he did this, all of his sins would be forgiven.

Just as the man was finishing the practice the saint came into the yard and inquired what the man was doing. Upon being told what the disciple instructed him to do, he blessed the man and walked into the ashram to find his disciple. When he found him he said, "Don't you realize that if you say the name of God with love, just once, it is enough to cleanse the entire kingdom? Why would you tell that man he needed to say it ten times? Do you have so little faith in the name of God?"

................................................................

Fr. Frahm married my wife and I in a little country church in South Dakota. It was a warm September afternoon, with blue skies and a steady gentle breeze that sang in the Cottonwoods outside. During the service, he was illustrating a point concerning what we needed to remember about one another with this story.

In the beginning, God and all the hosts of heaven gathered to discuss the creation. God felt uncertain about the best way to put things together and thought he should open the matter up to discussion. He asked many questions and gathered a great deal of information from those around him. When he came to his last question he asked, "Where will I manifest myself in creation that will not distract them from living their lives? As soon as they notice me they will never be free again." Many ideas were considered until a small angel in the back of the room said, "Why don't you hide inside the people? They'll never think of looking there."

Here are two more of Fr. Frahm's poems, from Summer's Lease:

<u>To Jesus On The Rood IX</u>
Jesus, I know there's more to you than crosses—
Risen Son of the mount's receiving cloud—
and likewise more to me than pain and losses;
still, here I bow as I have often bowed.
Nor is this symbol you, this graven thing.
Yet, wounded Savior, all-pervading Lord,
when neural pathways scream for solacing,
or inner tempest swamps your calming word,
(when my words blow like winds on a vacant ear),
then even tawdry tangible seems sweet;
and, much relieved to find you waiting here,
I stretch to kiss the silly plaster feet.
     For any sign, however mean, will do
     if it but bring me, gentle Lord, to you.

<u>Transfiguration</u>
These trees in fall,
bereft by frosts
of chlorophyll,
set forth whole feasts
called beautiful.

But what I see
is nothing new—
or so they say
who claim to know:

Golds are ingrained;
the red inheres,
masked by the green
through summer's hours.

Lovely it is,
yet sad if grand,
to be so teased
just as the trees
let loose their leaves,
and those who lived
seek out the ground.

(After winter
comes the spring.)

How strange God's ways.
For so it was
with those three men,
not being wise,
who yet caught sight
of God in Man
before He sought
Jerusalem.

They saw Him as
He always was;
their eyes opened
to let them find
the Who and What
in dazzling white
before the end.

    (After winter
    comes the spring;
    after Easter,
    everything!)

# Chapter Eleven

# Religion

In the early days of my relationship with Fr. Frahm, I remember asking him, "What do you think about religion?" He was quiet for a moment and then answered, "Useful but dangerous."

Fr. Frahm felt that given the right circumstances, a person's spiritual life would bloom in any religious setting. His experience, however, suggested that much of the time, religion interferes with our best opportunities for spiritual development. Fr. Frahm taught that spirituality is a deeply human and not at all a religious undertaking. Like all aspects of humanity, spirituality emerges from an individual's real thoughts, feelings and experiences. We cultivate spirituality not in a church, but in the human heart and human life. From there, it evolves and emerges into the world.

The danger Fr. Frahm spoke of is the strong tendency of religion to blur our spontaneous and deeply flawed relationship with life in which the seeds of real spirituality lie in wait. An authentic and imperfect encounter with life is a necessary element of spiritual growth. Religion has a tendency to bring the mechanisms of shame, guilt, judgment and orthodoxy to our encounter with the harder edges of our lives. These religious ideas, if we are bound to them, demand our attention and by definition our obedience. They distract us from the task of being who and what we actually are. Instead, we concern ourselves with what our religion believes we should be and what others say and think. When our focus is on dogma or religion rather than on what is honestly who we are and what we authentically think and feel, spiritual growth is difficult.

Religion traps you within a system of certainty that tells you without hesitation what is right and what is not right. Religion looks favorably on what it considers to be good and condemns what it considers bad. The problem is that we are human, and as such, are prone to make mistake after mistake. Through choice or error, the bad is where we will spend much of our time. Even when we do what we think is right, it is likely we hurt something or someone in the process. If we are only allowed to find God in the good, correct or acceptable, we miss all of the opportunities for spiritual growth that come with, and in, the bad.

You see, if God is everywhere and in everything, then we can find God in every mistake, poor choice, or violent act. Not beside you, carrying you or watching over you, but inside you even as you act. God is part of, and apart from, the very mistake you make. When we feel troubled or even tortured by our actions, Fr. Frahm would say God is as well. When we run from our feelings and into the arms of some compulsive behavior, God is there also. When we stare into the eyes of something evil or ugly, we look into the face of God. According to Fr. Frahm, when we cry, God doesn't cry for us, he cries with us.

Fr. Frahm would listen to people giving thanks to God and remark "It seems that God's always a winner." What he was saying is that God always gets credit for the successes. Whenever anyone win's, overcomes something or finds success they are quick to say that God was responsible. But you will never hear the words, to paraphrase George Carlin, "The good lord made me fumble." Fr. Frahm's point was that God must be right there, involved in the problems. If God's there, they are important to your growth and can never be rejected or denied.

Fr. Frahm remarked to me once, "You will never have a spiritual life until you can sin and still love yourself." Fr. Frahm worked very hard to teach people that they were free TO sin and even so they were still good people worthy of love. He knew that until people learned this, they would never be free FROM sin. And without this, spirituality of any kind would escape them.

The problem is that nothing in western religion or culture teaches us to sit with, hold, and give place to those less than perfect parts of human existence and of ourselves. When we cannot sit with these things and hold them in honesty, they haunt our every step and compel us to repeat them. Only when we can sit with what we have done and not done and accept what is, will we see God's fingerprints on everything.

There is the temptation to interpret what I am saying as some kind of conversion experience. But I'm not talking about "seeing the light" and turning to God. I'm talking about the idea that God lies at the center of the bad as much as He does the good. Fr. Frahm felt that whatever it is that created the universe has to permeate everything within it. This creator must lie within the people, objects, and events that we find troubling and even abhorrent. Our minds will always struggle with this problem because it is difficult to sit within our own fear, shame, guilt and self-righteousness and find compassion for what we are afraid of or what we have done, but it is there, in those dark corners, where spirituality can bloom brightest.

Fr. Frahm cared little for ideas like good and bad or right and wrong. He knew that these words mean only what people want them to and, therefore, they can never reflect who God is. "Beliefs, ethics, and morals are not bad," he would say, "but if they interfere with your ability to feel what is inside you or be honest with yourself, they are." Fr. Frahm believed that an honest assessment and experience of your real thoughts and feelings, not just the ones your religion approved of, was absolutely necessary for a healthy spiritual life. At the same time, he was quick to point out, that "just because you are feeling it, doesn't mean you should act on it. It is here that you should pause and just sit for awhile."

Religion is weighted down with a very clear picture of the way things should be; it forbids you from thinking, feeling, and experiencing certain things. Even more dangerous, religion prescribes what you should think, feel, and experience. It suggests there is no need to live, be authentic, and find these things out for yourself. You shouldn't see value in any process that doesn't reject sin or Satan. The church tells you what and who you are, so there is no need to engage in the trial and error process that brings about real learning. In fact, this type of behavior only leads to trouble for you or worse yet for the church. Just listen to the church, do what you are told, and everything will work out for the best.

This is a common form of religious and spiritual inertia that can't help but stifle spiritual development. Spirituality is an individual process, and religion is a group and institutional process. The more invested you are in the group, the institution, and its dogma, the less you can deviate from its pace, direction, and goal. In the end, you sacrifice individual personal spirituality for the certainty and safety of religion.

Religion also slows spiritual growth in a more covert fashion because, as Fr. Frahm told me repeatedly, "An individual with a mature spirituality will no longer need the church." Fr. Frahm saw in this problem a subtle and insidious movement toward dependency rather than freedom. He often remarked that if religion did its job, and set you free, the church would be empty. Churches are not built to be empty, and for the most part, they are not built to set you free.

In the last phase of his life, it seemed that Fr. Frahm had given up on the idea that religion of any kind could do the job it purported to do. Religion talks a great deal about freedom from sin and death but in reality does precious little other than to request faith in a symbol and a dogma that will be rewarded after death. He did not see this as the only option or as the best option. As I watched him counsel those who were having problems of faith and difficulties with religious beliefs, he appeared to me to be like the little Dutch boy sticking his fingers into the holes of a dike that was destined to give way. He would only talk for so long. Then he would remove his fingers, walk away and watch the dike burst.

I know now that the real value Fr. Frahm saw in religion was that it gave people something to rebel against. Fr. Frahm believed in rebellion as a pathway to spiritual growth and he knew that if nurtured properly, rebellion drives people to search out their own answers and consider other possibilities. Only in the midst of this rebellion, do people find the keys they need to free themselves of whatever shackles they might wear. Shackles such as, desire, fear, anger, abandonment, frustration, and self hatred are hard to slip. Some of us have been shackled so long we have come to fear the experience of freedom. In any case, we need all the help and luck we can get. Fr. Frahm's type of religion would tell us that we were imprisoned, support our rebellion, and encourage our escape. Most religious authorities would not see this as appropriate behavior coming from a cleric. I think he enjoyed this to no end.

Over his years of service as a religious functionary, Fr. Frahm learned that the Christian idea "have faith, do good, and all will be well; God will take care of you" did not seem to work well for the average Joe. I heard him say more than once, "That medicine will only work if you take it three times a day, every day, for the rest of your life, and even with that, good luck to you." He believed that what religion can offer will not sustain most people through the difficulties of life. And why should it? How can the complexity of a human life be endured through ideas like "have faith" or "God loves you" or "the Bible says you should do this"? These are not adequate answers; they are merely ways to avoid accepting the complex, absurd, chaotic, brutal, and mysterious aspect of human existence and finding God right there.

To answer the question of what to do, Fr. Frahm went as he always did to the great spiritual teachers, and primarily to Jesus. Again, he saw the lesson of Jesus' life as the idea that you could, in fact, live like Jesus in THIS life, and experience God each day. In doing so, you have no need for faith in an afterlife. Jesus seemed to suggest that religion or the Bible or faith cannot take the place of going inside yourself and looking directly at what you find or don't find there. Everyone goes into the Garden alone. It is what we find inside us that makes all the difference.

In the framework of religion, you need only have faith that Christ died for your sins. You do not have to actually do anything other than ask for forgiveness. This is a prescription for pain, victimization, and existential insecurity, as well as a gospel of despair. Jesus led a life of being and doing, without separation from God, but with complete unattachment to family, man, church, and state.

The life of Jesus exemplifies not faith, as the fathers of the early church were so desperate for us to believe, but a way of living every day that brings you closer to God on that day. Fr. Frahm felt that you had to go inside and address what was there before you could benefit from a faith of any kind. You have to go inside and assess issues such as guilt, shame, judgment, and fear. These are often the main boundaries that keep you distant from God no matter what you choose to do.

Fr. Frahm realized what all spiritual teachers realize. Regardless of what the Bible says, people cannot love anything or anyone unless they love themselves. How we love ourselves is exactly how we love others and how we love God. If the kingdom of God is within you and you don't love who you are, then God will always be distant from you. If God is within other people and you don't love them, then God will again be far away. Only if you love yourself, can you love others. If you love yourself and the others in your world, there will be no need to look for God because He will be everywhere.

Fr. Frahm said that the only thing that can fill the longing of a human heart is God. Not a belief, a religion, or a faith, but the experience of God right now. Religion can offer this, but it is often distracted and loses the focus it must always have...you and your God right now. Instead, politics, dogma, finances, righteousness, faith, sinners, different beliefs, sexuality, marriage, and getting to heaven too often take the focus.

Fr. Frahm took a different road and focused on the relationship with God that is available to you in this moment if you want it. Go inside each day and honestly get to know what's there. When you do that, your ability to love yourself will grow, and then eventually, your ability to love everything else will grow. As you learn to love your world, you will realize that everything you wanted was inside you all along. In this love, problems are not solved, chaos is not abated, absurdity not clarified, brutality not thwarted...In this love they are still everywhere, but they just don't matter as much.

In the fourth of his sonnets addressed "To Jesus on the Rood," Fr. Frahm writes:

> Some days your story seems to lack all sense,
> and more, offends a balanced sense of taste.
> Then reason arms for sanity's defense;
> doubt assays learning's gems to rid the paste.
> What of those tales told of a mangered hour?
> Of miracles? Of sufferings' relief?
> Of an empty tomb, that shored a system's power
> or stoked dashed hopes and, so, assuaged a grief?
> I question, Lord, until my strength is spent,
> my whirring brain is numbed, my faith dismayed.
> Yet, this one tale proud Man would not invent:
> a god made in our image thus displayed.
> > Wherever I pry, I spy confronting me
> > the scandal of all love pinned to your tree.

## Stories

The great thing about an idea, when compared to a belief, is that an idea can change and grow with the one who holds it. The following ideas are for you to think about. If they offer something new, please consider it for moment, not because my perspective on religion is correct, but because something new might emerge from inside you.

.......................................................................................

Overheard at a college lecture:
"Fr. Frahm, I was hoping to get your thoughts on a question."
"Go ahead."
"Could you define God for us?"
"Yes, God is that about which nothing can really be said."

.......................................................................................

A bill was proposed in Congress suggesting that the scriptures should be revised. Everything that leads to fear, anger, and exclusion should be examined. Anything that removes the dignity of even one human being should be deleted.

When members of the press discovered that it was Jesus Christ who had returned and authored the bill, they immediately asked him for a comment. He replied, "The scriptures are for human beings. Human beings are not for the scriptures."

.......................................................................................

Many of the people who came to see Fr. Frahm talked at length about sin. Some came to discuss it theologically. Some came to confess whatever sin they believed they had committed. I, having done both of the above, asked one day what sin was. Fr. Frahm looked out the window and said that he didn't really think much about it, but ultimately he was sure of one thing. The only sin that matters is thinking someone else is a sinner.

.......................................................................................

Fr. Frahm was always trying to get people to think differently about what they had been told about religion and about Jesus. Once during a discussion someone said, "Of all the laws these two things are significant: Love thy God with all thy heart, might, mind, and strength, and love thy neighbor as thyself." Fr. Frahm responded, "I am of the opinion that the Bible authors listed those in the wrong order because unless you can do the second, you can't do the first."

.......................................................................................

A young boy ran into his house in tears. His mother scooped him up in her arms and held him as he cried, "Please take it back, I just want to play." over and over. "It can't be that bad," said his mother, "what happened to you?" "I know who I am now," the child said. His mother looked at him and said "Jesus, that's wonderful." The child walked to his room and shut the door.

.......................................................................................

A great many of my interactions with Fr. Frahm involved me trying to deal with my past. Once, I confessed to a behavior which I was ashamed of. He listened patiently. When I finished, he was quiet. When he spoke he said two things. First, he looked at me and said, "Your problem is that you are a thief." For a moment I was confused, as my confession had nothing to do with stealing. "You have stolen something that belongs only to God and that is the ability to judge your soul. I have looked at today's paper and I did not see the notice stating that God had resigned and the company was taking applications to fill his position." He then suggested very directly that I should get out of the God business as I was unqualified to play God, with my own soul, or anyone else's.

Oh yes, the second thing he said was that the only one who can judge... doesn't.

One day before Torah/Talmud study, I overheard Fr. Frahm speaking with some members of the synagogue about the Holocaust and the nature of evil. An individual asked him why God would allow evil to exist in the world. He felt that, strictly speaking, this was a bad practice for any deity. Fr. Frahm looked troubled and was quiet for some time. When he looked up he said, "I guess God has a lot to answer for .... but then, so do we."

Jesus and Satan met one morning for coffee. Satan was having a particularly bad day. He spoke at length about mankind's attempts to make him responsible for things he did not do. He told Jesus that he had no real difficulty being the prince of darkness, but man was simply going too far. They were holding him responsible for evil they inflicted on each other. He had played no part in it. They suggested that he robbed people of their self respect when in fact they gave it up freely without consulting with him as to whether he wanted it or not. He looked to Jesus and said, "I can't work like this. I'm sick to death of being held responsible for things I did not do or say." Jesus looked at Satan, placed a hand on his shoulder and said, "I know what you mean; they do the same thing to me."

Fr. Frahm once said that mankind knows infinitely more about evil than Satan ever could or did. When I asked him to explain he said, "Nobody could ever damage your soul like someone who loves you...and Satan doesn't love you."

When my first child was born, Fr. Frahm gave me three pieces of advice regarding his religious upbringing.

1. Take him to church because he will need hooks to hang things on. This will serve as his compass later in life when he needs something to rebel against.

Again, it is Fr. Frahm's belief that religion can offer the keys to freedom, but your freedom does not lay in faith but in doubt.

2. Go to church with him so he knows that church is not just for children.

Fr. Frahm knew children well. He knew that if the parents don't take something seriously their child won't either.

3. Do not go to church every Sunday.

First, teach your child that Sunday is holy even if you're not in church. Then teach him that all days are holy.

................................................................

Quite often I listened to the conversations Fr. Frahm had with others who came to visit him. I remember one conversation with a particularly religious person who talked at great length about the miracle of the crucifixion. He was direct in his position that the miracle of the crucifixion was that Christ was divine and he allowed himself to die for our sake. I remember Fr. Frahm thinking for a moment and then telling this person that Christ, if he were divine, had certainty about what would happen after death. His only real concern would have been the physical pain of the crucifixion process. This is not a miracle. On the other hand, if a man named Jesus allowed himself to die because he felt it was the right thing to do, without any certainty about what would happen after death, then that would be a miracle.

# Chapter Twelve
# Not Freedom From, but Freedom To

The things in this life that are of any value have to be **given** and **received** freely. What I mean by this is that you have to give and receive with no expectation of gain or approval from the other person, the environment, the universe, or even God. If you give or receive in any other fashion, it is an attempt at control/manipulation. I will give you this so you will care about me. I will accept this from you, and you should do what I want. I give this to you because you ought to want it. If love is to set you free it must be given and received with no stings attached.

This issue of giving and receiving, according to Fr. Frahm, is spiritually important. Much of what we are taught culturally and religiously is based on the idea that you should perform/love/worship/honor/obey because it is wrong or sinful not to. You have been systematically instructed to come to the most significant activities in life from a place that stifles freedom. You love your God because if you don't you will not get to heaven. You love the significant others in your life because you want to be loved, valued, or noticed in return. Of course, each of your relationships should be bathed in love, and most of us work hard to give our love to these people. But the world doesn't encourage us to do it freely. Instead of nurturing a love that is free, our culture teaches the importance of meeting our own needs first. In the world we have created, love is largely an illusion.

Only when we give something freely can others receive freely. To receive freely means that you accept what is offered exactly as it is. You do not assume that, since he or she gave this to you, they will think, feel, or act in a particular way. Nor do you accept what is offered in an attempt to get the other person to do what you want at a later time. You just receive in thanks. We need to learn to accept without attempts to manipulate others into a desired feeling or action.

I became aware of this at lunch one day when my son turned a simple "thank you" into a performance in which he fell to the floor unworthy of the ice cream he had been offered. I asked him later why he behaved the way he did. He told me that he said "thank you" for the ice cream because he might have wanted more. He believed the best way to increase his chances for seconds was to be extremely thankful for the firsts.

Fr. Frahm taught that all things have to be given and received freely or they slowly lose their meaning and start a pattern of subtle dysfunction. To Fr. Frahm, your ability to love and your relationship with God were the most important elements of life. Therefore, he focused his teachings on the idea that God's love is given freely and needs to be received freely.

For some people, this idea can be strange and disturbing. Most of our religious teaching clearly dictates that you are to love God, no matter what. To do otherwise is seen as bad at best and sinful at worst. Yet, in the face of theology and tradition, Fr. Frahm said it didn't work that way. He taught that God gives love freely and that He wants us to do the same. To make his point he was very fond of saying, "Any God that does not give his love freely is not much of a God."

This idea started to make sense when I became a parent. When my children could openly and directly refuse to care about me, I had a choice. I could punish them and attempt to force them to love me or I could manipulate them to get the love I wanted. Presented with these options, I had to admit that neither of them originated out of love for my children. They originated out of my own pain and need to be loved. I could allow them to be free, within practical limits I set for them, or I could place my needs in front of theirs. If I am a parent, their need to be free to choose should come first. All I can do is set sensible limits and love them no matter what. At this point, I suspected that if I could figure this out, God could as well, and in fact, probably did long ago.

Fr. Frahm went to great lengths to teach people that they must also be free from each other. People should be in a relationship out of choice and not out of necessity or need. This becomes a difficult hair to split. Ask yourself, "Am I with him or her because I want to be, or am I with him/her because I am afraid of being alone, fear I will find no one else, or think I don't deserve better?" Fr. Frahm suggested that I, and everyone else, look closely and honestly at our relationships to see whether or not we are free and, if so, whether we are leaving the other person free. This is difficult to do for many reasons. First and foremost is the fact that if we lack freedom long enough we will no longer realize we are not free.

Fr. Frahm often repeated an idea he found in the poetry of E.E. Cummings when freedom was the issue. He would say, "Not freedom from, but freedom to." What Fr. Frahm was suggesting is that most of our freedom is freedom from. This is how human beings relate to the idea of freedom. Freedom, for most of us, only has meaning if it is freedom from some person, place, or thing.

Our freedom matters most when some "thing" comes along and places an undesired limitation on us. In the narcissistic culture we have created, we are told that nothing should in any way limit or control our wants, desires, and needs. We are constantly supposed to be going forward in a mad dash toward progress, gain, or whatever lies beyond the horizon. Fr. Frahm taught that most often, "freedom from" only allows us to escape ourselves, the very place we need to be.

There are cases in which "freedom from" is worthwhile, such as freedom from injustice or oppression. In these instances, Fr. Frahm's only concern would be whether or not this freedom brought you closer to the larger consciousness inside you. Freedom from oppression is a worthwhile freedom, but in reality, if it only serves the needs of your individual ego-self, then you must question its worth.

"Freedom from" something is most often a combination of thoughts and behaviors that serve the best interests of an individual ego-self. Although the ego-self has value and needs to be considered, it cannot serve as the driving force behind real freedom. If your freedom only serves your ego-self, than your freedom is largely an illusion.

Fr. Frahm suggested that "freedom to" does not serve only the ego-self. It considers the individual ego-self, but recognizes that other issues, egos, and perspectives need to be taken into account. It recognizes that our actions can be oriented toward something larger than our individual selves. With a larger picture that holds multiple points of view, "freedom to" can take people beyond the narrow confines of their ego-self toward the larger consciousness that runs through all things.

"Freedom to," because it does not have to protect the individual ego-self, invites us to slow down our self centered, forward progression through life and embrace our existence in this moment. We need not move beyond right now to be truly "free to" let go of what causes suffering and pain. "Freedom to" allows us to move beyond the illusions we cling so tightly to. This freedom does not require us to escape or reject any aspect of who we are. The only thing we need to do is consider other possibilities and a larger reality than the one we live in.

Fr. Frahm, didn't choose to see freedom as freedom from life, fear, pain, tragedy, sin, or any other ego-based concern. He chose to see freedom as an opportunity to recognize that the concerns of this life, although important, and real to the ego-self, are not ultimately significant. As he told me again and again, "It just doesn't matter."


**Exercise:** You can practice this exercise at almost any time. All of us have countless opportunities to give and receive things during the day. Each of these instances is an opportunity for you to better understand your own ego-self and to practice giving and receiving in freedom. Start with something simple that you do everyday. Getting a cup of coffee or some repetitive task at work will do just fine. Whether you are asking for a paperclip or hugging a loved one, your ego-self will operate in a very consistent manner. Practicing on a little thing, if you are aware, will teach you as much as the most significant events in your life.

Take a moment before you engage in your chosen experiment and breathe a little. Try to bring as much awareness to the situation as possible. This will help you better understand yourself. You want to experience how it feels for you to give or receive whatever you are involved in. What you think is also of some importance, but not nearly as much as what you feel. Consider what you are thinking but put it away for later.

Now just breathe, and with awareness, give or receive whatever it is. Move slowly and take the time you need to become aware of what is happening inside you. With every movement you make and every word you say, what do you feel physically in your body? Take a moment to feel it. Give it a name. Are you anxious, frustrated, angry, or dissociated? Just feel whatever it is. Then go somewhere quiet where you can contemplate it. Don't analyze it purposely. Just accept it. Allow your thoughts to come and go. That feeling may take you to another and then another. Who knows what will come into your head? Just follow it. Allow it to progress naturally. When it's done, it's done. Take what you have learned, and give or receive again.

Accept whatever responses come to you, but try to stay focused on your experience. Allow yourself to feel anything that comes into your awareness. When the encounter ends, naturally walk away. Go to a quiet place again and contemplate what you bring to these moments. What do you desire or need? What do you want the other person to do, think, or feel? Most importantly, can you feel your response to the moment and still breathe and be yourself with the other person? The goal is not to do away with some unwanted internal business. It is to acknowledge your business and remain yourself with the other person.

Work with this exercise. Cultivate your ability to recognize your responses, hold them, and remain with the other person. Learn to open yourself to him or her. Offer them attention and understanding no matter what is happening inside you. You don't deny your responses, but you don't have to allow them to drive you either. Study yourself, be present, and learn to give and receive freely.

Here is the opening sonnet from Fr. Frahm's sequence "To Jesus On the Rood":

> Jesus, I grieve when I consider now
> the sorts of streets my wayward feet have trod;
> and you -because you would not disavow
> your final promise, true kind Son of God -
> you walked beside me every bitter mile.
> Faithfully into darkness you came,
> stung by my sin yet quick to reconcile
> and slow to chide, most patient with my shame.

> Silent, you walked where angels would not go-
> into my hell, my loneliness, my pain;
> and to that end where such paths lead, I know,
> you went yourself that I might live again.
> Here to this cross, where I, forgiven, bow,
> my sin brought you, and your love brings me now.

## Stories

Fr. Frahm said that a good story is like a crowbar. If someone reads it and carries it around, he or she will ultimately pry their door open just a little. Once the door is not stuck, they can do with it what they wish. If Fr. Frahm was right about this, then a handful of stories could change the world.

Fr. Frahm and I were at the store where we met a friend of his—a clergyman. He talked at length about the difficulties of dealing with certain members of his congregation. One, in particular, troubled him. He announced that he was going to make a visit to his home to talk directly about saving his soul. Fr. Frahm was quiet for a moment, then he looked up and asked, "What are you going to do with that soul once you save it, collect the whole set and trade with your friends?" Then Fr. Frahm told him this story; it is a variation of one from Anthony De Mello:

A man was walking by a stream, and he saw a monkey thrashing around in the water and screaming. He watched the monkey for some time and discovered that the animal was taking fish from the stream, running up the bank, and placing them in a tree. The man walked up to the monkey and asked what he was doing. The monkey replied that he was saving the fish from drowning.

At this point Fr. Frahm told his friend that he would see him soon and began to walk away. He turned to me, shrugged his shoulders, and said, "It sounded like a case of monkey salvation for fish." In most, if not all cases, our position on what is true, correct, and/or helpful may work wonderfully for us but will ultimately take others to unhappiness and often, disaster. People need, as much as possible, to be free to be who they are.

One night over supper Fr. Frahm looked at me and asked if I knew why Moses never got to enter the Promised Land. I responded by saying that the story suggests he was being punished. He smiled and said that he felt it was the only way for the Hebrews to be free.

Moses had become the Hebrew's conduit to God. As long as he was there, the Hebrews would rely on him rather than on themselves. In order to free them, God had them leave Moses behind. "The purpose of your relationship with God is supposed to be your freedom," Fr. Frahm said, "but for most of us it becomes another form of bondage."

"This was also why God took Moses' physical body to heaven upon his death," he said. "If the Hebrews had his body they would bury it and build a shrine for it. Do you know what the problem with a shrine is?" "No," I answered. "Wherever you build a shrine is exactly where you stay. That's not freedom."

On one occasion, Fr. Frahm requested that I tell him how I understood what he had just said. I responded by trying to be funny and saying that his story was like a finger pointing to the moon. If I stared at the finger, I would miss heaven, blah, blah, blah. Fr. Frahm was never easily outclassed. He simply picked up what I had said and went on. "A belief is like a finger pointing to the moon. It is a hint, a clue to the mystery that will always be out of our grasp. Some people never get beyond the finger. Others like to suck the finger to make them feel better; these are the people who use God as fire insurance. Still others use the finger aggressively and gouge their own eyes out. These are the bigots whose beliefs have made them blind. Finally, you should know that those who stare at the moon and speak only of it, are called blasphemers."

Fr. Frahm and I were talking about Easter and the crucifixion story. I was unsure of its meaning and asked him to give me his thoughts and feelings. He said that if God were as bright as everyone seems to think, then He probably realized a long time ago that the only love worth having is from someone that does not have to love you. If I love because I'm afraid I'll be punished, that's obedience. If I love to get what I want, that's control. Love has to come from a person free to love you or not. In order for humans to be free to choose, God has to appear impotent, to appear to tie his hands and do nothing. The crucifixion was just one time when he appeared to tie his hands to wood with nails.

I often talked philosophy with Fr. Frahm. I remember asking him once if he had any notion of the meaning of existence. He raised an eyebrow and said, "You're assuming that existence has a meaning." I knew right then I was in for trouble. I mumbled, "I hope it does." Fr. Frahm said, "There is an important point here. When you learn to experience existence as it really is, rather than what you think about it, you will find that your question has no meaning."

# Chapter Thirteen
# Silent Laughter

Fr. Frahm was a contemplative, and as such, he was drawn to silence. The silence he loved so much was more than the absence of sound. He was drawn to a silence that has a content, loveliness, and a music all its own. He told me that his friend, Rabbi Balotnikov, said that the Torah begins not with Aleph (the first letter of the Hebrew alphabet) but with Beth (the second letter). Therefore, one could learn all of the scriptures, have great wisdom and still be ignorant of that long silence that was before the beginning. Fr. Frahm spent his days exploring this silence, and he fell in love with its song.

As with all elements of spiritual life, the only place this silence can ever be found is within. If you sit, quiet your mind, and slip free of the self you think you are, you might encounter a vast blissful silence. This silence is half joy, half consciousness, and half existence. It is the nature of that larger something that you step into during those moments of oneness when you forget the self you think you are. Think back to one of the brief moments when you were completely absorbed in your life and had forgotten yourself. It was quiet, wasn't it? If you were even minimally aware, you were in relationship to something very large and very silent. This silence is not a sound that you hear. It is an ocean that lies inside you, and you in it.

Fr. Frahm danced in this silence every day, and out of it, he heard love singing. In silence, he sang back. This is a difficult notion to wrap your mind around, and I must admit that I don't entirely understand Fr. Frahm's experience of silence. The silence within me is a joyous peace but it has only briefly been silent. And, as of yet, it has not sung to me. Maybe someday I will hear the silence he spent all that time talking about. Fr. Frahm couldn't get enough silence. He would frequently tell me, "The rule is not, do not speak, but do not speak unless you can improve on silence." In my experience with him, rarely could anyone or anything improve on silence.

He loved silence, but he also loved language because he knew how slippery words can be. Fr. Frahm taught that we use language primarily as a distraction, a trick. It is a method we use to control our world and keep others, and ourselves, from looking deeply at who and what we really are. If we keep speaking, no one, including ourselves, will know we are full of fear, chaos, longing and that abyss of terrifying silence. So we pretend, and we move forward pretending that we are reasonably stable and there is no need to panic. You see, most of us know the ocean of silence that lies within us. We have heard the waves crash on occasion, and although we have never seen it, we suspect that it lies out there just beyond the darkness. If we continue to speak, maybe we will never have to come in contact with all that silence.

People have called this silence many things: holy, Being, consciousness, nature, God. It doesn't matter what we call it. It very frequently terrifies us, especially at first. Terror is an honest appraisal of the situation, because silence is a double-edged sword. If we accept it, we will most certainly feel terrified by it initially because it threatens to engulf us. Most people, quite reasonably, feel that this type of encounter will overwhelm and even kill them, and in many ways, this is correct. That is the difficulty in dealing with this silence. To embrace it completely, not just listen to it, means something has to die. One cannot look upon the divine without first dying. So, few of us look. Our fear of a human death places us in danger of slow spiritual death.

If you do not approach the silence within you, you will remain fearful of it and never realize its actual nature. You will never come to understand its relationship to your spiritual life. If you have a spiritual longing, it can only be found within the silence at the center of your being. This is the truth of our lives. All pursuits, activities, and involvements that do not bring you closer to this silence can only take you further away from what you long for most, whatever that may be.

You cannot dwell in silence all the time because we need to communicate with each other to live our lives. But even when we are speaking to one another, we do a poor job of communicating, because most of us have lost any sense of connection between what we feel or experience and what we say. Our society, politics, business, religion, and ethics have created a culture in which we must fear what we perceive as not like us (particularly if it's unpleasant stuff). In so doing, human beings place themselves in imminent danger of abandoning the humanity of "the other." The "other" person, culture, group, religion or anything else that has become a "thing" to be feared. You must fear the "other" because its very presence threatens the position you accept as right, just, first, and correct. The longer you fear it, the more likely it becomes that you will lose the idea that the "other" is a valuable entity. Soon you will be justified in making the "other" into an "it" which is much easier to reject, destroy, dominate, and/or control.

Inside a world caught between fear, and its sibling, indifference, our words struggle to reflect our internal reality because this must be protected. Our words evoke no elements of our real humanity, which is constantly under threat. Trapped within this cycle, we speak not to know but to unknow. We design the things we say to provide safety and security rather than the real communication that is so necessary between people.

Fr. Frahm's intention was for your words to reflect your thoughts, feelings and intuitions. As we do this, our words can better reflect our true human content. With your language in relationship to your heart and your mind, others can see you for who and what you really are, and you can see others.

From this place, real communication can come about. We can open ourselves to others in honesty and acceptance, and from here we can feel and honor, violence, anger, fear, misunderstanding, and the interpersonal gap that separates us from each other. If you are willing to try to communicate with presence you may realize that language is often as much a hindrance as a help. In reality, very little is needed but authenticity and silence. Within silence, you can stop intensely being yourself, a father, a parent, a man, a woman, an American, a Democrat, a Republican, white, black, Asian, or native American, and just exist. Once you have abandoned these identities, you are closer to the place where only the divine is present and the voice of the holy is silence.

**Exercise:** This one is pretty easy, and I imagine that many of you have already anticipated a version of what I will ask you to do. The essence of learning about yourself is to sit in silence with the very things that trouble you. Do not attempt to overcome them or do away with them. Instead, sit with what troubles you and allow it to offer you a lesson about who you are.

Here, you will start to become aware of how you are silent. You do this by, yes, you guessed it, being silent. Find a quiet place, breathe, and come into silence and also stillness. Silence is the absence of talking but stillness is the silence of the physical body. Try to do both. Notice what happens. Most of you will get a quick lesson on how hard it is for you to be silent and still.

It is likely that your mind will not sit in silence. You may have already noticed this if you have tried some of the previous exercises. When you stop talking, your mind will actually increase its internal chatter. The more you focus on silence the less silent the mind becomes. The same is true for stillness. Sitting in stillness will make you very aware of your physical tension and your need to discharge your physical energy through movement. To what degree you experience both of these phenomena depends on what you bring to the exercise.

Relax a moment and remember that no one will do this well when they begin. Practice is the key. Take time each day to sit and be silent. Empty yourself with each breath, and when you struggle remember that no matter what happens, it's all right. Just return to your breath. Let all your tension and internal dialogue slip away. With practice you will experience silence and stillness and with this you will learn something about silence, love, and peace.

It strikes me as more than just a little ironic that I'm about to present a group of stories to help you understand silence. Even funnier is the fact that I'm going to use the most slippery language I can think of to point at an idea or two.

Maybe you're sitting there, as I once did, saying to yourself that you don't really get the point of all this. What in the world does silence have to do with God, spiritual freedom, or any of the topics at hand? I offer you the following stories. I hope they contain an idea or two that will answer that question.

## Stories

Fr. Frahm talked often about the importance of silence. He not only talked about it, he practiced it as well. He believed that the language of God is silence. When someone had difficulty with this idea he would often tell them this story from Stephen Mitchell (1991).

Sinai

Everyone knows what happened at the bottom of Mount Sinai, but no one mentions what happened at the top. In a way, this is unavoidable: the eye can't see itself, the equation can't prove itself. Nevertheless, a few of our sages have spoken. (In order to say anything, they had to be there.)

Rabbi Levi said, "On the top of Mount Sinai, Moses was given the choice of receiving the commandments or seeing God face to face. He knew that he could not see God without first dying. It was like looking into a mirror with no reflection inside."

Rabbi Ezra said, "Moses did receive a commandment, but only one, only the First. All the others blended into silence, as all colors blend into white."

Rabbi Gamaliel said, "Moses received only the first phrase of the First Commandment: I am the Unnamable."

Rabbi Elhanan said, "Moses saw on Sinai what he had heard from the Burning Bush. There was just one message: I am."

Rabbi Samuel said, "Not even that. The only word the Unnamable whispered was I."

Rabbi Yosi said, "In the holy tongue, I is anokhi: aleph-nun-koph-yod. What Moses received from God was the first letter of I."

But aleph is a silent letter.

Rabbi Yosi said, "Just so."

To give you another idea about how Fr. Frahm understood silence, here is another of his poems.

### Silent Music, Silent Laughter
"Where do you go when you fly up?"
        I asked the shooting sparks.

"To that same lair where notes lie up
   before they hunt their larks?"

Then lovely silent music burned
   the symphony of after
  and faded, composition learned,
   to joyful silent laughter.

...................................................................

Fr. Frahm often told me stories he felt I should hear. The trouble was that he would tell me the story, and then he would go silent as to its meaning or importance. One day I said to him, "You are always telling me stories but you rarely, if ever, tell me what they mean or what I am supposed to get from them." Fr. Frahm said, "How would you feel if I invited you for supper and then chewed all of your food for you before I put it on your plate?"

...................................................................

Fr. Frahm worked with deaf children when he went through seminary. He loved using sign language and had followed the exploits of a gorilla named Cocoa. Cocoa the Gorilla was one of the first animals to learn a workable amount of American Sign Language. Cocoa had accumulated a vocabulary of about 200 words and could carry on an elementary conversation with almost anyone. Cocoa began her training by learning the most simple and usable words in the English language, namely 'yes' and 'no.' Fr. Frahm loved to tell this story to people and then ask, "Do you know what the first thing Cocoa did with the words she learned? She told a lie."

...................................................................

I remember Fr. Frahm telling me constantly that inside silence was peace. He would admonish me to remember that if I sought to protect my ego, silence would only disturb me. One day, when he was in a mischievous mood he bade me goodbye with the following benediction: "May the silence of God disturb you always."

...................................................................

I walked into Fr. Frahm's home one evening, and he was watching the television. This was extraordinarily rare for him, and I asked what he was watching. He replied that Yahudi Menuin was playing. I replied that I had never heard of him. He said I should sit and watch. After the concert was over he said, "You should know two things. First, Yahudi Menuin is the most wonderful violinist in the world. Secondly, you need to realize that the finest words never come from the tongue."

# Chapter Fourteen
# Free Love

Fr. Frahm lived his life being and teaching love. His primary concern was always whether or not **you** felt **you** were worth loving. If you felt that you were worth loving, ultimately, you would love yourself. If you loved yourself, you could love others. And more importantly, you would not NEED others to love you. If someone asked me to summarize what I learned from Fr. Frahm I would look at them and ask, "Do you feel that you are worth loving?"

Fr. Frahm was an expert at finding ways to love people who made this task extraordinarily difficult to do. He could accept almost anyone for who they were, good and bad. And because he could accept the whole person, he could love them with ease. The roots of his ability to love others lay in the fact that he had a concrete sense of himself as imperfect and paradoxical. He had looked at himself with a profoundly fierce honesty and he understood what he saw to be deeply wounded and flawed. He embodied the concept that good people do bad things, bad people do good things and that he was both of these people...as are we all. He not only embodied this notion, he lived it. And he went to the length of writing it on the end of a hammer and pounding it into the heads of those of us who were "resistant."

When you sat with Fr. Frahm, you felt the genuine honesty with which he looked at himself and his life. This simple act was, for most people, enormously helpful and freeing. Fr. Frahm had no time for professional boundaries or thera-peutic disclosure. He was a loving presence that allowed others the experience of watching and listening as he shared stories of his own life and felt real feelings as he did so. There was no psychotherapeutic re-hashing of his past, there was only an honest human being who showed you how you could look closely at the worst parts of yourself, take ownership of them, and live through it.

The experience of witnessing Fr. Frahm own the truth of his own life was to know that you could look directly at all the pain, anger, hatred, abandonment, and aggression within yourself, take it all into your heart, and not be destroyed by it. If you looked into the abyss, if you ate the fruit of the tree of good AND evil and realized you would not die, you were free, free to love yourself no mat-ter what your feelings, thoughts, history, and sins had been. Once you are free to love yourself, everything else, and everyone else, will spontaneously become loveable.

Fr. Frahm saw within human relationships the opportunity to practice loving and being loved by God. To engage in this practice, however, he knew that you must be free to love yourself. Without feeling that you are worth your own love, the attempt to love anything else is useless. When you love yourself, you are free to love others without expecting anything or needing anything in return. This type of love is given freely, and thereby leaves the other free to love you, or not. Fr. Frahm believed that God loves you and I in this same fashion. You are free to love him or not and no matter what your choice is, his love remains. This is the love of a true parent, a creator God that wants you to grow and be who you are, not who or what he wants you to be. This is a truly human love. God may have created us in his image, but it is possible that he learns about love from us.

Fr. Frahm often said that the reason God created man was not to be worshiped but because He desired to love and be loved. Even God could not give himself the experience of being freely loved. God wanted an opportunity to be in relationship with beings that could choose to love or not, and He could choose to love them. Within this kind of relationship everyone grows. I think it is likely that God grows as well. Of course it doesn't always work out like this, but that is also part of the bargain.

"There are as many ways to God as there are people on earth." Fr. Frahm would say. He believed whole-heartedly in helping people find their own way to God where they could stand in relationship to him or her in whatever way was effective for them. Common paths to God include service to others, devotion, physical work and knowledge. For Fr. Frahm, the way to God was through love. His love was a deep, constant devotional love. He spent many years loving and making love to God through contemplation, meditation, music, and poetry and these years ripened his love for God. By the time I met him, he had stopped loving and had become love. He embodied a deep love of God that was present constantly. He no longer loved or made love to God in any specific or defined way. He had become a loving poem that was read with each breath. Here is an example of his prospective on love from Summers Lease.

<u>"Love Is The Whole And More Than All"</u>
To spend and, in the spending,
    never count
        the cost;
to lose and, in the losing,
    not to hunt
        the lost;
to gain and, in the getting,
    question not

> the gift;
> to give and, in the giving,
>     deprecate
>         regrets.
> So love, and-in the loving-
>     nothing but
>         rejoice;
> and sing, and-in the singing-
>     not protect
>         the voice.

**Exercise:** It is important to learn about your own way of loving and any baggage that might be connected to it. As with all spiritual matters, daily practice is the key, and with it you will begin to understand your ability to love. As you go into this exercise, try to remain mindful of the lessons you have learned so far. Honesty, spirituality, freedom and silence all play a part in your ability to love and be loved.

Before you make any attempt to cultivate awareness of your existence, you have to start with some basic awareness...as always. You should take a moment to breathe and relax. In fact, now that I bring it up, breathe and relax every time you think of it. Living your life with awareness rather than distraction will be of infinite value to you if you do nothing else.

It is quite a wonderful thing to go from loving God to making love to God. Making love to God requires much less talk and much less doing. All you need to focus on is your present moment relationship to God and your participation in this relationship as a loving partner.

Find a quiet place to sit and breathe. Bring a symbol of God into your awareness. Whatever symbol you chose is fine. With no talking, prayer or other mental gymnastics, in any way that seems correct for you, embrace your God as you would a lover. Stand, sit or lie with God as you would with someone more precious to you than life itself. Just be there and love. Do not speak. Just be in the moment.

Attend to your reactions and file them away for later. Whatever comes up is important, but put it aside and focus on the matter at hand. Some people say they feel silly or even stupid doing this exercise. I have found that these people usually have great difficulty relating to God in any way other than a cognitive one. If God is only an idea or mental construct to you She or He will never be real enough to make love to. If this approach works for you, that's great. Who am I to judge? But it seems inadequate to me.

Work with this exercise in any way you wish. Be spontaneous just as you would with your real lover. Learn to fall to the ground and love in a way that completely erases you from the world. Here are two more suggestions about how to do this. Both suggestions are poems that I think make this point better than I can.

> Batter my heart, three-personed God: for, you
> As yet but knock, breathe, shine, and seek to mend;
> That I may rise, and stand, o'erthrow me, and bend
> Your force, to break, blow, burn, and make me new.
> I, like an usurped town, to another due,
> Labour to admit you, but oh, to no end,
> Reason your viceroy in me, me should defend,
> But is captive, and proves weak or untrue,
> Yet dearly' I love you, and would be loved fain,
> But am betrothed unto your enemy,
> Divorce me, untie, or break that knot again,
> Take me to you, imprison me, for I
> Except you enthrall me, never shall be free,
> Nor ever chaste, except you ravish me.
>
> *(John Donne, Divine Poems 14: 1971)*

> <u>The Heart is Right</u>
> The
> Heart is right to cry
> Even when the smallest drop of light,
> Of love,
> Is taken away.
> Perhaps you may kick, moan, scream
> In a dignified
> Silence,
> But you are so right
> To do so in any fashion
> Until God returns
> To
> You.
>
> *(Hafiz, The Gift: 153, Ladinsky, 1999)*

## Stories

Fr. Frahm expressed his love for others through story. He gave you a story as a gift for you to keep and play with. I asked him once where he got his stories. He responded by saying, "When God wants you to be a student, he sends you a teacher. When he wants you to be a teacher, he sends you stories."

Fr. Frahm talked with many people about their difficulties parenting. He was always concerned about the child's ability to love him or herself. He believed that if a child cannot love himself or herself, they cannot love God. When talking to one individual he said, "The real difficulty in the life of a child is not that they are not loved. The real problem occurs when they come to believe that they are not worth loving. Children have a great deal of dignity. If they think they are not worth loving, they are unlikely to waste their own love on themselves." The person with whom he was speaking with became very quiet. Fr. Frahm looked at him and said, "You see, if I don't love myself and you tell me you love me that leaves me with two choices. First, if you can't see me for what I know I am, then you are a fool. I don't need any fools for friends, thank you very much. Second, if you are not a fool and you still say you love me, then you must want something from me. At that point, I have to keep one hand on my wallet and one hand on my balls. How can I embrace anyone from that position?"

Fr. Frahm asked me once how I could tell if a person was enlightened. I said something like, "He would be at peace." Fr. Frahm said "No." "He would have no fear of death," I said. "Nope," said Fr. Frahm. Finally, I was frustrated and I said, "So tell me." He leaned toward me and said, "An enlightened person will look into the face of anyone and recognize someone he loves." If you can look into the eyes of a stranger and love what you see, no matter what it is, you are free. But, more importantly, you set him free as well.

Fr. Frahm was speaking to a friend of his who was very unhappy. His friend spoke at length about his girlfriend and the difficulties they were having. He said that he tried so hard and did everything he thought she wanted. But still, she was distant and cold. He feared that the relationship was over. Fr. Frahm said, "It sounds to me like you think you have to earn your love." His friend was quiet for a moment and then responded, "Yes, I suppose I do." Fr. Frahm said, "If you think you have to earn your love, you will never be able to. And love that you have to earn isn't really love."

# Chapter Fifteen
# Judgment, a Cautionary Tale

Much of the pain and suffering we experience is brought about by our compulsive need to judge ourselves and then, of course, to go about judging others in the same fashion. The problem imbedded in this process is the fact that when we judge ourselves or others, we almost always condemn, regardless of the situation.

This need to condemn is a compulsive practice. It is compulsive because we are most often unaware of our real thoughts and feelings or unwilling to honestly examine them. We either can't, or won't, look at what lies within us because we are afraid of it. Unwilling to look at our real thoughts and feelings and afraid of what lies within us we have to condemn ourselves. Without an acceptance of self and the understanding that this brings, we are quick to project this unwanted material onto those around us and we condemn them as well. This dynamic requires that we condemn almost everything. Although this process has many contributing factors the most important is the needs of the ego-self.

The ego-self is awash in a sea of anxiety. It has brief periods of relative calm, preceded, and followed, by mild insecurity or outright fear. The threats posed to the ego's constructed sense of security are numerous. Any encounter with the unknown, unwanted or uncontrolled can, and usually will, increase the sense of insecurity experienced by the ego-self. Our ego-self must be thinking, feeling and doing what it defines as safe and correct in order to be secure. The threat of the uncertain and having to accept responsibility for our choices looms larger with each new experience we encounter. Therefore, one of the best ways to foster security is for the ego-self to clearly label any, and all, other positions, opinions or actions as highly suspect, regardless of what available evidence might suggest.

It's a fact that some opinions and actions are more valid than others. When you evaluate your actions or beliefs, the evidence needs to be considered, and reason should be employed to determine the justification for what you do or don't do. Fr. Frahm, however, was concerned that if the individual is not aware of, or can't tolerate, the anxiety generated by their own threatened ego-self, he or she will feel compelled to judge in order to relieve this anxiety.

For most people, this process of threat, anxiety and judgment occurs well below their level of awareness. It is unconscious, instinctive and, therefore, habitual. Almost any perceived threat to the ego-self, no matter how superficial, engages this drive to judge and deny responsibility. If we feel driven to judge by our anxiety, then all evidence, whether in support of, or against the issue, (the position of the ego-self), will largely be ignored. Therefore, unless we directly acknowledge the ego-self, and the compulsion that emerges from it, our judgments are likely to be compulsive/habitual and not based on sound reasoning.

Fr. Frahm suggested that judgment often becomes a habit, and will continue until a loving human presence offers an alternative perspective. This new perspective must be more than a theory about other people and why they behave like they do. It must consider other people, yes, but it should look at the individual doing the judging first. The only way we can change something as fundamental as our process of judgment, is to recognize that our own needs and desires lie at the bottom of it. Unless you honestly look at yourself first, nothing is likely to change.

The distinction that Fr. Frahm said we have to make, regarding judgment, is between the judgment of the person, and the judgment of their behavior or action. Fr. Frahm felt that we could judge the behavior and actions of another, as long as we are being honest with ourselves, and the other person. If we cannot look clearly and honestly at what we do, think, and feel then we should probably avoid the judgment altogether. But under no circumstances did Fr. Frahm believe we were to ever judge the human being.

The judgment of behavior is part of our social contract with one another. Our legal and political systems are designed to make judgments, right and wrong, about what is good for us individually, socially and culturally. These decisions form the foundation of our ability to live peacefully and productively with one another.

However, Fr. Frahm was very concerned that this process was easily corrupted. Not so much from the legal or political position, although that did concern him, but primarily from the individual position. Our personal process of judging others is built upon how we judge ourselves. Fr. Frahm was concerned that if we judged ourselves compulsively without using reason, this method would spill out onto our judgment of the behavior of others without our even being aware of it.

The manner in which we judge ourselves is essentially the same manner in which we will judge another. If you don't like you, or can't accept parts of yourself, or refuse to honestly look at who you are, or refuse to be responsible for your own behavior, thoughts and feelings then this is exactly how you will judge another. If I don't like me, I won't like you. If I can't accept certain things in myself, I won't be able to accept them in you.

Fr. Frahm felt that if you intend to engage in the judgment of another, you need to look inside yourself first. You need to honestly and carefully look at what you actually think about you. You need to look closely at your own process of judgment and what you bring or don't bring to it. Fr. Frahm felt that this is not something you can do in a thoughtful moment. If it was this easy to examine ourselves and make changes, we would have fewer problems to start with.

We should look at our drives, and needs, as well as the evidence for what we do, think and feel. Finally, even as we judge, we need to remember that the difficulties with judgment are largely unconscious, and therefore, difficult to see. Fr. Frahm felt that if we started here, we would be less prone to judge unfairly or dishonestly, and possibly less prone to judge at all.

The judgment of the person was quite another matter for Fr. Frahm. He was very direct with his admonishment that we needed to be very cautious about judging the person. Even in cases that we consider to be extreme, such as serial killers or rapists, he felt we needed to be cautious; not because our judgment is wrong, but because our judgment is easy and feeds the ego-self and its compulsion to be God-like. The more we are driven to judge, the more unjustified our judgment is likely to become.

When I say to someone that they are entitled to judge the behavior of another, but not the person, they frequently nod in the affirmative and say, "Of course," as if this is what they and everyone else has been doing all along. If we are honest, however, we know this is not always true, maybe even rarely so. We don't usually make this distinction, and I think Fr. Frahm wanted us to consider whether or not we are able to make it at all.

We slide so insidiously from the judgment of behavior to the judgment of the person that there is cause to be concerned any time we judge another. The process happens unconsciously in most cases, and often, we aren't aware that it took place at all. Deep within us, the ego-self becomes involved and acts in a self-serving manner. As long as we have not started to properly address the ego-self, and even after we have done so, judgment will be tricky and we should be cautious.

I realize that this position will rub some people the wrong way. I have heard the responses before. "Some people are just bad people." "We have to look for what is wrong in other people and judge the wrong as bad." Although these statements have some truth in them, they also have within them the voice of an ego-self that doesn't want to give up its ability to judge others because it needs to do this in order to be secure. All Fr. Frahm ever asked of anyone is that they think about this before they climb to the top of their moral, ethical, or religious high horse.

There is one more aspect of judgment that Fr. Frahm was quite concerned about, and it is forgiveness. At the very beginning of forgiveness is one important pre-forgiveness activity: you have to judge the other person as having done wrong. In other words, if I forgive you, I have already judged you as wrong and in need of my forgiveness. Fr. Frahm did not feel that forgiveness, as an idea, was bad or in some way flawed. He had simply learned that some people like to forgive because they enjoy the judgment that comes first.

He encouraged those who came to him to look closely at how they forgive and what part judgment plays in it. Fr. Frahm felt that if you were going to forgive someone, you needed to examine yourself first. If your forgiveness is nothing but an opportunity for you to be better than someone else, it actually degrades everyone involved. If your forgiveness is a method of control, again, this is not good either. One last point he often made about forgiveness is that, without a prior judgment, forgiveness is pointless. Without judgment, there is nothing to forgive.

We engage in far too much judgment, and we do it in a very dishonest and unjustified fashion. Fr. Frahm felt we needed to look at ourselves, and honestly inquire about what we're doing and why we're doing it. He felt that we needed to become aware of our ego-self and the problems it can cause. As we begin to do this, we may discover that we need to judge less, and when we judge less, we may possibly learn more. I think he was hinting at this idea in his Sonnets to Jesus in Summers Lease.

<u>To Jesus On The Rood, VII</u>
Once again has a friend of mine betrayed-
one whom I loved the best and trusted most.
For this our old relationship is frayed:
A confidence I lent he spent in boast.
Then word got back to me, and I was hurt
To learn afresh a lore I thought I knew:
that friends on earth will, soon or late, desert
and, of all friends, my one fast friend is you.
Jesus, I blush to bring my rankled pride
To one who knew the sting of Judas' kiss
and whose sad eyes still blessed when friends denied.
Forgiving Lord, instruct me more in this:
    How unself-righteously to pray, with you,
    "Father, forgive; they know not what they do."

**Exercise:** The best way I know to deal with the burden of judgment and the issue of forgiveness is to change my orientation toward the other person. Everyone in your world that has done wrong to you, or has in some other way missed the mark that you believe they should have hit, can help you with this. Each of the people that you would normally judge, consciously or unconsciously, has been trying to teach you something. They have offered you an important lesson about who you are and how you engage in relationship with others. By changing your orientation, the people you are driven to judge can be your teachers.

Pick someone that you don't approve of in some way. This person may have done something to you, to someone you care about, or who may be completely removed from you. It doesn't matter. Just be clear on what your problem is with them. Now sit, breathe and become present. See them sitting directly across from you. Now breathe, and be with this other person. Come into silence and find some comfort with this process. When you are ready ask yourself "What has _______________ taught me about myself, what has she or he given me?

This is a place were you need to have a fierce kind of honesty available to you. Otherwise it is too easy to just brush them off and say they have taught or given you nothing. People are only mirrors. We know nothing of what is inside them therefore we see only parts of ourselves that we project onto them. How does that person make you feel? What does that have to do with who you are?

Maybe that person reminded you that you shouldn't take your anger out on anyone. Maybe you learned that a lack of humility causes problems. Perhaps you should remember to think before you react. Or, possibly, you should focus on not putting your needs ahead of other people. No matter what the lesson, you owe that person a debt of gratitude, not judgment. They have, through their own pain and suffering, offered you the opportunity to look at yourself again. They remind you to take care of your own business before it gets too large. They plead for you to ask for help.

Those you would judge are your teachers. Each of them suffers for you so that you have one more chance to change your own life before you miss someone else's mark. Sit with that person and find the lesson. Be honest with them and be honest with yourself. The opportunity to learn is right in front of you if you can step away from your ego long enough to seize it. Now you owe them thanks, rather than judgment.

## Stories

At a gathering of parishioners, a woman began to talk about her son. This woman was a devout Episcopalian and Fr. Frahm had known her for years. She had gone to some lengths to raise her children to be good Episcopalians and good Christians. Her eldest son had moved away and had fallen in love with a Jewish girl. This did not trouble her at the time, but he had since announced his intention to marry her. This woman was beside herself because her son would have to be married in a Jewish synagogue with no real Christian marriage ceremony. Worse yet, he had discussed with her his thoughts about converting to Judaism. She looked at Father Frahm and said "What shall I do?' He thought for a moment and said, "If Judaism is good enough for God's son, it's probably good enough for yours."

Fr. Frahm always told me that any judgment we make, whether person, thing or behavior, is a judgment of something created by God. I talked frequently with Fr. Frahm about the Sermon on the Mount and the beatitudes. One day, we were talking about the section that states "anyone who lusts after a woman has already committed adultery in his heart." My feelings on the matter were that life is complicated enough. This type of thinking was just not helpful. Fr. Frahm said, "The issue here isn't the lust. The issue is that if you lust after her this lust takes place between your left ear and your right. The lust you feel is what she becomes. In doing this, you never know who she really is. The problem with lust is that it disregards the humanity of both of you. She goes from a person to an "it", and you made her an "it." We should worry more about who she is rather than what we believe her or want her to be."

...............................................................................

The apple had fallen to the ground. Adam and Eve hid themselves because they realized they were naked. As they hid, they heard God walking through the garden calling for them. He soon found them hiding in the tall grass. He looked at them and realized what had happened. He said to them, "Who told you that you were naked?" Adam pointed to the apple and replied, "She gave it to me." Eve replied, "The serpent tricked me." God looked down and went off to find the serpent. Soon, paradise was gone.

This is often understood as the moment of original sin. I would suggest that if there is anything we can call original sin, it is not disobedience. The sin we all carry and willingly repeat is the human process of judgment and condemnation.

...............................................................................

Fr. Frahm had little time for people who wallowed in self-pity. When someone stated that they had been hurt or wronged he would often say, "Getting hurt is nothing unless you insist on remembering it."

...............................................................................

I was talking to Fr. Frahm about my past. As always, he listened carefully to whatever I said. This time was different, however. Usually, he would listen to me with a look on his face that was almost pure compassion. By the end of this discourse, there was no compassion in his face. He said, "You know we talked about this before." I said I knew that but the issue still troubled me. He leaned back and said, "When I was a parish priest I would take confession daily. Over the years of doing this I feel that I have learned a thing or two about people. One of the things I learned was that if someone confessed to the same sin more than twice, it was useful if I accused them of bragging."

I learned two very important things that day. First, no matter what I had done, I had not reinvented the wheel. Second, God did not think I was the center of the universe, and neither should I. No matter what I have to say, God has heard worse and more interesting.

........................................................

The Bible tells the story of the woman caught in the act of adultery and was going to be stoned. Jesus arrives and suggests to all those present that he who was without sin could cast the first stone. While everyone thought about what he said, he went off by himself to write on the ground. Soon all the accusers were gone. I have always been interested in what he was writing or drawing. Some think he wrote down the sins of the accusers. Some think he wrote down the sins of the woman. Still others think he felt awkward and was doodling. I think that the most important thing about what he was writing was that he wrote it in the dust of the ground, where after only a short time, it would certainly blow away.

# Chapter Sixteen
# The Sound of Death

Fr. Frahm's spent his life searching for God. He looked in all the usual places and tried all the usual activities and then ultimately, he found God in the only place God ever could be, inside his own heart. His discovery was one of experience rather than the product of faith or a construction of the intellect. Once he had found God, he simply let go of his self and walked into God as one would walk into the ocean. Living a life this close to God allowed him to exist with very little fear of death. The fear of death had become unnecessary, because his death would set him free.

There is a point worth belaboring here. Again, it is the idea of experience. The religious dogma surrounding faith exists for the sole purpose of filling the hole left by the lack of honest human experience of the divine. Our culture and history have little time for the idea that we can experience God as a feature of daily life. Because of this, we are left impoverished with only faith in an after-life to sustain us through the difficulties of living and dying.

With no experience of the Holy to tie us to what is real, the pending storm called "death" blows us in every direction until we finally run and shelter ourselves within a dogma that promises protection. Fr. Frahm said that no dogma was necessary, what you needed was an experience of God. If you cultivate this experience, even death can't move you from Gods' loving presence.

When I experienced Fr. Frahm's death, I learned that how you live and more importantly how you live your death is as important, and probably more important, than what happens after you die. Much speculation and theology exists to address this question even though it can never really be resolved. No matter what crystal ball we gaze into, what book we read or who returns from the "great beyond" with an interesting tale, we will really never know what awaits us. Without an experience of something eternal, you have no choice but to fall back on faith. And when faced with something like death, faith is a poor replacement for experience. With this in mind, it does little good to ponder the issue at all. The only thing that can and does matter is how you live.

Fr. Frahm said repeatedly that the real message of Jesus did not concern religion or the afterlife. It was a direct and obvious lesson on how to live each day in the presence of God. It was also a lesson on how to die in the presence of

God. Fr. Frahm said that if we went to the scriptures and studied these two ideas, completely disregarding the notion of what awaits us after death, we would find something important. Love casts out fear, even the fear of dying.

According to Fr. Frahm, our fear of death, and our desire to be rescued from it, is a fog that lies over our vision of what is real. Two things are real, this moment and the essence of the divine that runs through it. This individual moment, the one you have right now, is all you will ever have. This moment is your opportunity to see God in everything and see everything in God. Your life is an eternal invitation and opportunity to be embraced by the divine. Ironically however, this can only happen if you are authentic and embrace your life with love...even the parts that frighten you or the ones you don't like. To live in fear and deny this life in favor of an afterlife is to leave God's most precious gift unopened.

Fr. Frahm taught, by example, that it is possible to live and die with no distance from God. He did this through love, and there was no need to speculate on what happens afterward. Fr. Frahm had considered the matter but was able to die without having the intellectual mystery solved. Or maybe he had solved it for himself but never discussed the matter with anyone else. Regardless, he died trusting his own heart and, in doing so, trusting his relationship with God. I will leave you to sort this matter out for yourself, with the words of Lao-Tzu:

> The Master gives himself up
> to whatever the moment brings.
> He knows that he is going to die,
> and he has nothing left to hold on to:
> no illusions in his mind,
> no resistance in his body.
> He doesn't think about his actions;
> they flow from the core of his being.
> He holds nothing back from life;
> therefore he is ready for death,
> as a man is ready for sleep
> after a good day's work.
>
> *(Tao Te Ching, 50, Mitchell, 1991)*

When Fr. Frahm arrived at the hospital he pulled me aside and asked me if I would be his medical power of attorney. He explained what he wanted and didn't what to happen when his death came close. In the end I agreed to everything he asked and promised that I would protect him. He needed this promise because although he was not afraid of death, he was afraid of the medical indignities of dying and the problems that inevitably arise between people confronted with a dying loved one.

I did everything I could for him to insure that his death came quickly and painlessly but I couldn't stop the people from coming. So many people came to say goodbye. His room was constantly full of family and friends. Even when Fr. Frahm was no longer conscious he was never alone. People came to talk to him, say goodbye or just see him one last time. As the days past Fr. Frahm was no longer responsive but his vital signs changed little. I started to be concerned for him because I couldn't understand why he didn't leave us. And I knew he wanted to.

Then I remembered many years before talking to him about a patient I had who waited until I was on vacation to refuse dialysis. After two days he was gone. When I returned I was confused about what happened and why my patient had made the choices he made. Fr. Frahm listened to me and said, "Sometimes people are unable to let go. They may want to die but they feel they can't if the people around them aren't ready to let them go. Others don't want those they love to see them die. Dying is something you have to do all by yourself and if you can't let go, you suffer."

That evening I went to Fr. Frahm's room and did the hardest thing I have ever done. I told him I was leaving him and I told him goodbye. I asked the others if we could leave him alone for the night and it was decided that only his youngest daughter would stay. I went to Fr. Frahm's home and went to sleep for the first time in two days. Sometime after 1:00 am the call came. He was gone.

**Exercise:** We will always avoid the places that scare us. Death scares us, and we naturally resist an experience of this fear. After all death comes soon enough in this life. Yet, I'm going to ask you to sit with your fear and learn about your relationship to it. For most of us this is easily done. Plan to have some free time and travel to the cemetery of your choice. Stand at the gate and begin to breathe. Once you are aware of what is happening inside you walk around. Look, really look at the graves. See what is written on the stones. Stand, breathe, and feel a stone. Whatever comes up for you just smile, have compassion for yourself, and breathe. After some walking find a comfortable spot in the grass and sit. Breathe and feel the grass. See the stones, and be aware of what arises in you. Are you fearful or anxious? Do certain memories come to you? Do you envision the suffering of the future? Do you fear your own death? No matter what comes up, breathe, and with honesty accept it as part of yourself.

The idea of this exercise is to cultivate a tolerance of your finiteness. You cannot control it or hide from it. It is a fact of life. If you work with this issue long enough, I hope that you will learn that there is only right now, and to experience right now is to experience the eternal. Yes, you are going to die, but the sun is still warm and the wind still blows. Even in the face of death, this moment will always be beautiful if you have the courage to live it.

There is a Native American saying that I try to remember: Have courage, only the earth lasts.

## Stories

We were talking about death and what happens after death. Fr. Frahm always had very little time or interest in these questions, but I wanted to hear what he had to say so I pressed him. He thought for a moment and said, "Most people treat the afterlife like they treat their Christmas presents. They pick them up, shake them, listen to them, and try any number of tricks to determine what is inside. If you think God loves you, then you will have to trust that he doesn't give junk as gifts. If you are going to trust in the life He gave you, you will have to trust in the death as well. As for me," he said, "I think that the One who gives IS the gift."


Then we sat and he read for me his Sonnets to David, of which three are included here.

> I
> Oh, dear, dear friend, who could have thought as much
> some twenty years ago or thereabout,
> that I'd walk limping, propped by cane or crutch,
> and cancer's winds would blow your candle out?
> This we have learned since we left school behind:
> life's ablest teacher, cold Experience,
> imparts hard lore and little of it kind,
> that rare commodity, uncommon sense.
> She seldom taught of self-forgetful love-
> foolish, perhaps, by some thought dangerous;
> but such we had, nothing to gain or prove,
> and such will have as long as we are us.
> > She well could learn what we have come to know:
> > beyond my love's long reach you cannot go.

> VI
> Knowing the blest exist and you are blessed,
> having that hope confirmed past reasoned doubt,
> in short, a faith beyond the dreamed half-guessed
> are certainties I've had to do without.
> But well and good; let hope suffice for me,
> such as it is and wanting sureties.

I am somehow offended when I see
folk taken in by cozy sophistries.
Convinced of bliss to come, some are so sure
that all is well they wait in apathy;
in evil's grip they count themselves secure
and abrogate responsibility.
    Since God made heaven, too, that's His to give;
    but let me seek His Presence while I live.

<u>VII</u>
But let me seek His Presence while I live,
and for the rest I am content that He
design our end to His prerogative,
unmoved by nagging fears from such as we.
Yet grant those trusting souls all they believe,
and I'll suspect the total gift, when given,
will render finally speechless tongues naïve,
so beautiful, so vast a state is heaven.
And if I had to guess or theorize,
I'd hazard this which cuts my mind adrift-
it is too huge to grasp or realize:
that He who gives is in Himself the gift.
    If that's the goal toward which your life is drawn,
    your death entails no night, but breaking dawn.

Ultimately, faith is of little use unless it develops into simple human trust. If you trust in the life God gave you, you must trust in the death he gives as well.

It was June, I think. That summer was a blur, really. I had brought Fr. Frahm lunch because he had been ill for some time, too ill to go out. He looked across the table between spoonfuls of hot and sour soup and said, "I don't think I will be around much longer." I knew him well enough not to argue, so we spent the rest of lunch talking about his death and the process of dying. He told me what he was mainly afraid of the indignities that doctors and hospitals inflict on the ill and the dying. After hearing him out I said, "And you're not afraid?" He reached for a manila envelope on his shelf, pulled out a manuscript that was to become Plains Songs and read this to me.

Prescription: Chamomile Tea,
To be taken half an hour before bedtime on winter evening

Here is a poor man's rich wine,
the sherry-golden
chalice prince
ale-disguised in peasant gown.

Oh, it is air distilled
from mown hayfields
off on the farms of young;

The speckled brown
of a pheasant hen
sitting her nest
by a hedgerow,
the eye cocked upward yellow;

the smell of fresh loam
                              thrown
from the badger's burrow;

grasses, straw, trees,
all of these,
their stems and leaves
and fragile flowers.

It is the gnarled old Yellow Transparent
harvest apple in blossom,

the snowdrift bloom
of wild plums
massed along fencerows,

a nickel from Grandfather
for a whole
pack of spearmint gum.

It is springhouse water,
cool, clear, moss-edged,
shaded from June sun
by a roof shingled in cedar;

and, the ladlehandled enameled
drinking cup that hung

to welcome all comers,
friend or stranger,
its sole requirement
a parched tongue
or a droughty throat;

the sweet scent
of honey
pressed new from the comb,
a winter evening way
to taste
the bees' song
at noon.

It is wrenburble
from the clothesline,
slow turtledove cooing
from the Scotch pine,
the grackle's
rusted-gate-hinged
creaking.

It is the raincrow's call
half an hour
              before
thunder;

and, the drops
that fall
        down
                under
honey locusts
after the clouds have gone,
and the sun shines again
seeking
the pure light azure blue
of tiny butterflies
at puddlecongress
after rain.

Oh, it is wind-chafed cheeks
and blond curls,

starched pinafores,
clean patched overalls,
school lunch pails

(emptied syrup cans
with stout bails)
and pintopound
on gravel
off to school.

Yes, off to school and
abc's
penmanship, ciphering,
the merry-go-round,
Annie-over-the-coalshed,
the swing,
"fill your head
with everything
just be home
by choretime."

It is clean
white muslin sheeting
bleached on gooseberry bushes
in raw March morning sunshine.

It is lying
at last
after dark in haytime,
the east window open,
listening,
        hearing
the mockingbird still singing
somewhere in the row
of Osage orange
a quarter mile away.

And it is waking
                Later,
somewhat nearer dawn,
to the gentle scent

and the sleep sound
of soft rain on the hay.

"Do you know what this poem is about?" He asked. I said no. He smiled and said, "It is about my death."

..................................................................

As Fr. Frahm lay dying, I spent most of my time talking to those who had questions about his health and what has happening. As time moved forward, I became more aware that many people could not handle the fact that he was dying. It became clear that some people, understandably, needed him too much to let him go. I had some quiet time with him, and I said "Many people are struggling with what is happening to you. I'm really worried about a couple of them." He looked at me and said, "They'll get over it...or not." He said nothing more about it.

At the time, I thought he was simply frustrated. God knows he had every right to be. Later, I realized that he was just stating things as they truly are. No matter what happens to us, it really makes no difference. The only thing of any real importance is between you and God.

..................................................................

Fr. Frahm always said that God was a mystery. I asked him at the end if death was the only way to know what the mystery was. He said, "No, you can sit in silence each day. If you do it well enough, you can dissolve into the mystery without having to die." I smiled and said, "Like the sleep sound of soft rain on the hay." He leaned forward, touched his forehead to mine and smiled.

# Chapter Seventeen
# Prayer and Other Forms of Hypocrisy

Fr. Frahm taught a great deal about prayer, but little about the act of praying. He believed that how you prayed and what you said while praying was inconsequential. The only thing that mattered was that you prayed. It was your choice to pray and the act that followed that made all the difference. Prayer, as he saw it, was standing before God with thankfulness and love. What you said was not terribly important. Your decision to be thankful and loving was.

Fr. Frahm repeatedly said, "Prayer is not desired or demanded by God, but it's very important to the process of being human." Although he believed that what you said while praying was not that important, he felt that much of what we spent our time saying to God did not bring us any closer to him. For many of us our prayers are only a laundry list of things for God to do. Help me do this. Bless her while she does that. Forgive me my other thing. "If God is half as smart as people think He is, Fr. Frahm said, He will likely treat our prayers in the same way we treat junk mail." Oh, another letter from him...and then, a thumping sound as it hits the bottom of the trash. Prayer is something we need to approach with more authenticity and honesty but much less talk.

Fr. Frahm told me several times, "Prayer changes people, not God." Prayer is an opportunity (without wordy dialogue) to place oneself before God (whatever God is) and express love. From this place, we can quiet the ego. In silence we can find peace and the opportunity to better see what is real. More importantly however, only when the ego is quiet, will we ever hear God.

The opportunity that lies within a prayer is the possibility of losing your everyday ego-self. It is an opportunity to shed all the things you think you are that stand between you and God. It is this ego-self that places us at the center of the universe where we become the most important thing in existence. Whatever we place at the center of our universe is, by definition, God. This is not something we do purposefully, but the fact remains that our survival instincts and psychic needs are so strong we habitually become God.

This identity we think we are has to be shed or at least loosened up a tad. The voice of the self that reports, explains and justifies our thoughts and feelings to us must be quieted if we are to make a decent attempt at real prayer. Without working toward losing ourselves, our prayers become directives from the ego on how the universe should be run. Even if we throw a "your will be done" or a "in Jesus name" in at the end, it is unlikely that God is fooled.

The problem with dialogue oriented prayer is that words most frequently come from the ego. Our ego-self has to be engaged, on some level, in order to speak. This self tends to pray with its own best interests in mind whether that self is aware of it or not. With this risk always present, silence is the best and ultimately most useful option.

In silence, we are nothing but a humble and thankful being before God. We can express love without diluting or confusing it with garbage. This is one of the most significant personal sacrifices you can make. You sacrifice your need to talk. You give it up as an offering to God. Maybe your God requires more than this, but I can't imagine why. A being that has taken the time to express thankful as well as sacrificing its need to make a case for itself has offered something unimaginably large.

If we are silent we have a much better chance of slipping our collar and running off to play. You see, in prayer, we can be humble and thankful but we can be playful as well. The primary feature of play is the complete loss of the self. Play, intentionally or unintentionally, is a prayerful activity. The question then, is do you pray as if it you HAVE to pray, or do you run and dance like a child? If you are dancing, then the definition of play and of prayer is very similar. Prayer can take the form of playing with children, serving others, singing, gardening, washing a car or mowing the lawn. In fact there is nothing that cannot become prayer if you are willing to get out of the way.

This problem goes all the way back to the beginning when two people named Adam and Eve were not content to play with God in paradise. They fell because play wasn't enough. They took the apple and with it their egos emerged, and life became a serious business. Each of them experienced the emergence of a self that needed to be significant and secure. They were no longer satisfied with play.

Any negative connotation attributed to the idea of play reveals less about play than it does about the one who attributes it. Our problems with play are essentially our problems with prayer. What stops us from being able to do either is our sense of self-importance, our need for others to see us in a certain way and our need to control.

Fr. Frahm prayed very little when I knew him, and I now realize why. Just as he had figured out how to become love, he had also become a prayer. He laughed as prayer. He ate as prayer. He loved as prayer. His life had become a prayer offered to God, some good and some bad, and because of this, it was perfect. Here in this Sonnet to Jesus is a something of what I mean.

<u>To Jesus On The Rood XI</u>
Jesus, I sometimes fret that I rely
too much on you, but am I fit for weaning?-
since you, and only you, can satisfy,
and you, and only you, give my life meaning.
When I do try to go it on my own,
I reel like a crippled tot and err and fall.
Thus, I have learned I cannot walk at all.
Let folk deride such need for props as weakness;
I still will choose, as my dependency,
that rood whence you depend-all strength in meekness,
for you alone both lift and leave me free.
     Enough of kneeling, Lord, enough of talk.
     Now make your cross my crutch that I may walk.

**Exercise:** An activity I like to recommend to those I work with is that they offer themselves as a prayer. Find a place to sit. Breathe until you feel calm and present. Now, with each breath, fill your body with thankfulness. Each time you inhale, allow the beauty and wonder of the world to ride your breath into your heart. Each time you exhale, allow what's in your heart to overflow into your whole body. In silent stillness, fill yourself with thankfulness. In whatever way makes sense to you offer this to whatever God you worship. Just be thankfulness and peace. Like a hum or a subtle vibration, emanate this prayer into the world. If you hear any internal dialogue just breathe, and return to your sense of peace and thankfulness. After you have sustained this for awhile relax, lie back and rest. What is different about you now? What is different about the world?

## Stories

I was attending a public function with Fr. Frahm. The person in charge offered a prayer. The prayer was very dramatic and was something of a performance piece that seemed a little over the top. I spoke to Fr. Frahm later during the meal. I told him that the prayer seemed a bit much to me and I wondered what he thought about it. Fr. Frahm said, "He who prays so that others will hear him has his reward."

Fr. Frahm liked to tell the story of the dervish who was asked why he worshiped God through dance. "Because, "he replied, "to worship God means to die to self. Dancing kills the self. When the self dies all problems die with it. Where the self is, God is not." Nothing more true has ever been said.

........................................................................

Fr. Frahm was speaking to a group about prayer. He discussed what prayer was or should be and how it could be done. At the end of the discussion, he told them to always remember there are four levels of prayer: First, you talk, and God listens. Second, God talks, and you listen. Third, you both talk, and you both listen. Finally, neither of you have to talk, and neither of you have to listen any longer.

Then he read this from Summers Lease.

<u>Meditatio</u>
Thy kingdom come,...How gracious,
   magnanimous of me,
    to kneel and (see how humbly!)
     speak the enabling word
   that gives such kind permission
    to all creation's Lord.

Thy will be done...How trusting,
   generous, cool and wise
   to close my curious eyes
    in knowing attitude
  and accord the Uncreated
   so wide a latitude.

On earth as it is in heaven....
   The phrases strike me dumb;
  and deafened, blinded, numb,
    I rise amazed to feel
  that I am in the bargain:
   the goods, the trade, the deal.

........................................................................

A young man asked Fr. Frahm how to pray. Fr. Frahm would not answer him directly, but told him the following story.

Two men were walking back to the house after fishing. They were tired and decided to take the short cut across the cattle pasture. Soon, after they jumped the fence, they discovered that someone had let the bull into this same pasture. They ran for the other fence but soon realized they were not going to make it. One looked at the other and said, "Quick say a prayer for us." He shouted back, "I can only remember one prayer." His companion said, "Just say it." The first man said: "For what we are about to receive, may the Lord make us truly grateful, amen."

Father Frahm looked at the young man and said, "Do you understand?" The young man smiled a little and shook his head no. Father Frahm said, "You will be truly praying if everyday you can wholeheartedly give thanks for the bull."

．．．．．．．．．．．．．．．．．．．．．．．．．．．．．．．．．．．．．．．．．．．．．．．．．．．．．．．．．．．

My experience with Fr. Frahm has led me to one conclusion regarding prayer. The only prayer that we have any chance of speaking with no hypocrisy or dishonestly is the following: "God, Thank You."

．．．．．．．．．．．．．．．．．．．．．．．．．．．．．．．．．．．．．．．．．．．．．．．．．．．．．．．．．．．

I walked into Father Frahm's home and he was very excited. He asked if I had time to sit with him and watch something on television. He told me that PBS was running his favorite ballet with Barishnakov as the lead. I looked at him strangely, because I had never seen a ballet nor did I really wish to. We sat on the couch and he turned to me and said, "You have said many prayers and you have heard many prayers but tonight you will see one."

．．．．．．．．．．．．．．．．．．．．．．．．．．．．．．．．．．．．．．．．．．．．．．．．．．．．．．．．．．．

Fr. Frahm loved to tell a story he heard from Rabbi Bolotnikov.

A cobbler came to his Rabbi and said, "I don't know what to do about my morning prayer. Those that come to me are poor and have only one pair of shoes. I get their shoes in the evening and work on them until morning. When the sun rises, there is still work to do if the men are to have their shoes before they start work. What should I do about my morning prayer?"

"What do you do now?" The Rabbi asked. "I try to rush through the prayer quickly and get back to work but I always feel very bad for rushing. Other days, I am so busy I am not able to pray at all. On these mornings, I know I have lost something. I often put my head down and weep. The Rabbi said, "If I were God I would value those tears more than any prayer."

# Chapter Eighteen
# I Play, Therefore I Am

*"There are two types of truth. In the shallow kind, the opposite of the
true statement is false. In the deeper kind, the opposite of a
true statement is equally true."*

Neils Bohr

Fr. Frahm laughed beautifully and he laughed often. Even though he felt
your relationship with God was the most important thing in your life, he never
took it so seriously that it was beyond laughter. In my years with him I came to
realize that he was serious about spirituality only for the benefit of others. He
knew that the challenges of developing a spiritual life often made it difficult for
people to laugh about the task at hand. For Fr. Frahm, a spiritual life was more
like play.

Play is an activity in which you let go of the ego-self and step into a much
larger world. It is larger because serious play requires you to be who you are
and to be something else as well. The act of play is not specific to this OR that.
Play requires this AND that. At play you can be in contact with your individual
thoughts and feelings AND, if you do it well, with that larger devine consciousness that is within and around you all the time. This, coincidentally, is also a
good basic definition for love, prayer and freedom.

Play is a state of freedom in which you must be part of life rather than its
observer. Freedom requires that you experience, and respond to, the present moment rather than encountering it as something that is unconnected and often a
burden or a threat. In play, your responses to life events emerge naturally from
choice and intuition rather than the compulsions and habits of the mind. At play,
your responses can be creative, spontaneous and authentic rather than a product
of what you need to feel secure at that moment in time.

But the greatest gift of play is that it allows you to embrace a wonderfully
human ability: the ability to hold multiple truths. One of the constants of human
existence is that we will encounter things in our lives that we will not identify
with or want to accept. These things appear to be completely unconnected and/
or opposed to who and what we are and believe. When life brings us experience
which is outside the world we subscribe to, overwhelming emotions, chaos, and

dis-regulation often follow. To achieve a level of safety and security, we quickly come to identify one way, our chosen way, as the only correct position. This is a type of fundamentalism and it will insure that anything natural, spontaneous and different is feared and either completely controlled or rejected. With fundamentalism as our safety net, we come to fear the natural flow of life, which is different in every moment. Then we have no choice but to close ourselves off to the larger space of play.

If one way is correct and all others are wrong, we see differences as irreconcilable. The possibility of relationship between multiple truths and multiple positions is forbidden. Significant relationship and communication in spite of difference is disallowed because the position of the other truth(s) is invalid. Thomas Merton (1964) stated that all oppression, whether self or other, is built on the concept of the "irreversibility of evil." Once a thing is wrong, or bad, it will always be so, and we then have a duty to reject or eliminate it. The results of this type of fundamentalism includes self-hatred, interpersonal violence, oppression, and on a large scale, war. There are, of course, cases in which war or violence are justified actions. Fr. Frahm's concern in this matter was that we should look closely at ourselves and question the justifications for our fundamentalism.

In today's world, we have a shortage of people who are able to hold multiple truths. You need only turn on your television to see the constant examples of this spiritual fundamentalism playing itself out with plenty of suffering and pain to go around. Fr. Frahm taught that spirituality, real spirituality, is about an individual holding two or more truths that seem contradictory and then allowing them all to exist as valuable pieces of his or her world. He suggested that this is an effective pathway out of self-hatred as well as interpersonal, intercultural and geo-political violence and injustice.

To step in this direction, all you need to do is entertain more than one truth, more than your truth, with genuine honesty and curiosity. Fr. Frahm had complete trust in the idea that if your attempt was genuine, you would learn that virtually all truths have something to offer. They may not be your truth but that doesn't mean you can't learn from them. Not only can you entertain multiple truths, but you can encourage and invite more truths. The more truths you engage, the more you will learn.

All deep human experiences like play have as a necessary feature the holding of multiple truths simultaneously. The idea that there is no need to adhere exclusively to one fixed and correct truth is the birth place of deep human spiritual experience. Play is probably the easiest and most effective way to interact with the ultimate mystery of God, and all of His or Her truths, without being paralyzed and forced into some ego driven fundamentalism for security.

Fr. Frahm believed that life is, at its core, a mystery. He saw life as a riddle in which the punch line is promised but never delivered. From this perspective life itself becomes a kind of play. If you can view life in this manner, play becomes a legitimate way to seek God. Play brings with it a state of being unfixed, logically illogical and without preconceived notions. In this wonderful state, we can look at things differently and allow something new to touch us. Without a state of openness like this, very little learning of any kind, spiritual or otherwise, is likely to occur.

Play brings with it freedom - freedom of the mind and heart. Laughter at the self, the world, and even God, provides a way to endure the pieces of our lives we cannot understand and make okay. Play is a kind of kneeling and laughter is a prayer. It is the song the soul sings to God. Here, from Summers Lease, is Fr. Frahm playing.

<u>The Almighty</u>
"Almighty God is subtle,
　　but He is not malicious."
He's also mighty playful,
　　but never mean or vicious.

By this we know He's caring
　　of men and smaller fishes:
He's bountiful in sharing
　　but slow to grant our wishes.

**Exercise:** I don't want to give you an exercise for this section. Play is not, and can never be, an exercise nor can it be forced or required. So rather than going directly to play, let's try to become aware of what prevents you from playing right now.

Stop what you are doing, take a few breaths and look around. Just breathe and bring a little awareness to the moment. Whenever you are ready, go to your kitchen and find a spoon. You will need a regular metal spoon, not too large. The smaller your nose the smaller the spoon should be. Feel free to get a handful of different spoons as some will probably work better than others.

Once you have your spoons find a chair and sit upright. Take a spoon and breathe on the concave surface until it appears foggy. Now try to hang this spoon on the end of your nose. Some of you may have done this yourself when you were younger or possibly you saw others do it. Rest assured it is well within the realm of possibility. It requires only a seriously playful attempt...or two.

As you prepare for this activity and even do it, breathe and become aware of your thoughts and feelings. What is preventing you from taking a few moments to play? Do you feel silly? Do you have other things you should be thinking about right now? Notice what arises and then breathe and go back to your spoons. As you play, try to become aware of what holds you back from enjoying the moment.

I must be honest. This exercise works much better if you do it with someone else, particularly a child. But doing by yourself is the best way to look at what is within you. Work with this exercise until you find yourself playing without planning or encouragement. Play with your friends, your children, and particularly your spouse or significant other. Hopefully, you will discover that you have a real gift for this.

## Stories

Each Thursday Fr. Frahm attended Torah/Talmud study at the local synagogue. Once, after study was complete, refreshments were served. He was given a dish of a wonderfully sweet, cold soup that I discovered was made of prunes among other things. Fr. Frahm turned to the Rabbi and said, "I assume this is the substance Moses our prophet was speaking of when he told Pharaoh to let my people go."

................

During his reading Fr. Frahm came upon the following verse. After contemplating it, he felt the need to comment. I found this in his notes.

> You sweep men away in the sleep of death; they are like the new
> grass of the morning, though in the morning it springs up new, by
> evening it is dry and withered.
>
> Psalm 90: 5-6

Marginal Gloss on Psalm 90: 5-6
I'd guess the psalmist, dead and gone,
had no crabgrass in his lawn;
else he'd have used, for you and me,
a very different simile.

................

Fr. Frahm always required me to think differently about life and things spiritual. I struggled a great deal to get past my own set habits of thinking. Even the simplest of spiritual options often escaped me. Once he asked me if I knew what the sound of one hand clapping was. I laughed and said I didn't know. He said most people never think beyond the question. What you should be asking is what the other hand is doing that it deserves such applause.

................

One day while we were discussing the Sermon on the Mount, I read the sentence that states, blessed are those who hunger and thirst for righteousness, for they will be filled. Fr. Frahm responded, "Blessed are those who hunger and thirst for righteousness, for they will get a belly full of it." When I looked confused he said, "I have noticed that those who seek righteousness look most critically into the lives of others rather than into their own."

I once asked Fr. Frahm about speaking in tongues. He replied with facts about its place in church and theological history. He spoke about gifts from God in both the Christian and Jewish traditions and how speaking in tongues fit into these systems. When he was finished I asked him what he personally felt about the practice. He said, "God gave me only one tongue and that gets me in quite enough trouble, thank you. I tend to think people should focus on better communication with one another in English before they start speaking in tongues."

Fr. Frahm also liked his humor with a touch of seriousness. One day he told me this joke: One day, two people walked into a church. One came back out, the other one drowned.

At a poetry conference, someone asked Fr. Frahm for a definition of Christian. I think they expected an answer based on theology. Many faces in the room changed when he gave the answer. "Christians are people who talk a great deal about love and very frequently hate other people."

Fr. Frahm and I were speaking about faith, as we did quite often. Our conversation became serious. It seemed to me that the question of faith was a life or death issue. I read, contemplated, and tried to live what I understood faith to be. These extravagances seemed to amuse him at times. During a particularly serious moment I quoted a Bible verse stating, "Faith without works is dead," or something to that effect. He responded without even looking at me, "I've often thought that the rest of that verse should read, 'and faith without humor is deadly.'"

# Chapter Nineteen

# Nature

It is a vast understatement to say that Fr. Frahm loved nature. It was the air he breathed, and even its smallest change never escaped his notice. He embedded himself within the natural world, and his sense of season and place were the coordinates by which he mapped his life. He seemed to not so much watch nature, as belong to it.

It was as if he was just another tree or flower moving through the yearly cycle of life. He came from the earth, and ultimately he would happily return. For Fr. Frahm, a separation from the earth and its cycle was tantamount to a separation from God. He felt God in the movement of the day and the passing of the seasons. He heard God in the sound of water and always in the wind. Animals, birds and butterflies danced for him at every opportunity and he was forever their thankful audience.

Nature had become his church. He lived within a world-wide cathedral that was always in the middle of praise-filled hymn. By the end of his life, he had left the stone and wooden churches completely in favor of larger and less orderly surroundings. In his backyard or looking out his window, the day's service was always in full swing. He loved nothing more than to walk outside and join the choir every chance he had.

Fr. Frahm was a gardener. His garden was of the English style, full of boundless flowers, specifically roses with such interesting names as Mr. Lincoln or Alexander the Great. His flowers were interspersed with things like Apple Service Berry, Joe Pie Weed and Shasta Daisy, their sole purpose being to entice creatures into his garden. The entire project was designed to bring birds, butterflies, and all manner of life to visit him. They all came, and brought a family of squirrels and two quail along. He created his garden to be sat in, walked in, and looked at. But more than this, he designed it to be felt and interacted with.

Fr. Frahm treated his garden as both sanctuary and classroom. It was a metaphor for human life and just sitting in the midst of it would teach you lesson after lesson on how to be alive. For instance, the wooden fence that surrounded his garden safely contained the feelings and thoughts expressed within, and it held back a large patch of raspberries bent on world conquest. The fence was high enough to slow the wind and rain and protect the flowers inside. But it was not near high enough to deter anyone or anything that wanted in.

Roses were everywhere, as many colors and varieties as he could find space for. Each rose beckoned to be observed in a way that would offer you a very obvious experience about the beauty and pain of life. Purple cone flower and Shasta daisies loomed in large patches, proving to everyone that while the cultured hybrid struggles, the brave and ragged thrive. In one corner, pansies trust their faces outward where they were beaten by wind and rain; each one remaining faithful to its purpose until it was finally wiped away.

The north wall served as a background for tall Asian lilies that dared to stick their heads out above everything around them. Placed strategically in the west were three beautiful peonies with no earthly business in that garden. They each glowed with their own fabulous deep green individuality. Precisely in the center of all this, as if placed by mathematicians, stood a single tall tree. It was a beautiful full Maple, round and even.

Just like the very first garden, this one too had a tree of knowledge, but it bore no fruit at all and that was the point. The meaning of the fruit has always been overstated. Our problems are not caused by Satan's trickery or Adam and Eve's choice to eat the fruit. They are caused by what happens in the human heart. What was the knowledge that Fr. Frahm's tree offered? To this day, it issues a warm invitation to sit in the shade and find out for yourself.

All of this was a Garden of Eden where one needed only to be still, and possibly, you would hear the voice of God. You would be loved, nourished and satisfied just as the birds and butterflies were. Just standing in the garden you would fall head first into creation and if you wanted, you could loose yourself completely. Fr. Frahm once told me that the reason man was thrown out of the Garden of Eden was because of judgment. Therefore, if you would simply stop judging yourself and others, you could walk back into the garden any time you wished.

Fr. Frahm's garden heard numerous confessions and was watered by countless tears. It survived and managed to contain the worst anger humans could generate. It also supported and fed those who had fallen so far they could no longer find the light. The garden was an extension of Fr. Frahm himself, and to this day it still feeds the souls of those who are lucky enough to visit.

Fr. Frahm knew nature to be the silent witness to who we are. It does not judge or control. It has no agenda or desires. It is the model of how life should be lived. Fr. Frahm taught that when we go into nature and sit quietly, we might glimpse what we really are and in doing this, we move closer to God.

One summer day, I approached the back gate to Fr. Frahm's garden. I could hear him talking to what I took to be numerous people, asking them about their day, and if they would like cookies. Lucky me I thought, as I lifted the latch and wondered aloud who had come to visit him. I opened the gate, announced myself, and the whole garden fell silent. I looked at the table, and looking back at me was Fr. Frahm with about six birds, two squirrels and one bunny rabbit all sitting or standing around him. It looked to me as if he was hosting some sort of party.

When I walked in the whole party stopped. All the animals turned to look, and then scattered in all directions. Some ran off with a cookie in their teeth. Some left their snack on the ground. Fr. Frahm sat in silence and watched them go. Realizing what I had done, I walked in, sat down and stared at the ground. I still remember the look of sadness on his face.

To this day, I am not sure what I witnessed. I have tried to host that same party, in that same garden a couple of times. To date, only one of the squirrels will come, and never too close. He appears, stands on his hind legs and waits for me to throw him a cookie.

The only way I can share with you what Fr. Frahm taught about nature is to take you to his garden or offer you a few of his poems. I will do the latter. Take whatever you learn here and go outside. Here are two poems from Summers Lease and one from Plains Songs.

<u>Aspengold</u>
I would not trade this sight of aspengold
on autumn mountainsides for anything!
The rubies of an oriental king
could not suffice for payment, were it sold.
The time may come when I am hungry, cold,
in want for comforts only coin can bring;
I'd still not sell this treasure, but would sing
in penury of wealth I now behold.

The memory of the bright loveliness
will be both bread and clothing to my soul,
a store against the future's leaner days.
But, come what will of poverty, distress,
I am recipient of this rich dole,
and shall remember it with grateful praise.

<u>Something Old, Something New</u>
The Elderberry, to speak her marriage vow,
wears veils of Cluny White upon her brow,
as Nature, nervous Mother of the Bride,
insures all customaries are supplied.

Although they seem to some like superstitions,
she nonetheless insists on all traditions.

The wedding guests were sent their invitations
and, punctual, come to take their honored stations:
Aunt Vervain, Cousin Asclepias are there
wearing the hues that older women wear;
while here's Queen Anne herself, in fragile laces-
beside her, Black-eyed Susans' cheerful faces.

And just as fragrant, yellow-clad Sweet Clover
wages her head in the hope "She'll think it over."
Here comes the Bride! So fair to look upon,
attended by her Maid, Erigeron,
and having on, around and all about,
accoutrements no bride may do without:

For Old, the gentle hills beneath make do.
And New? The month, for June's forever new.
The Something Blue, a high clear vault that lingers,
and Chickory's eyes, put in with smutty fingers.
(I must confess that it was I who threw
the single shiny Penny for Her Shoe.)
And what is Borrowed, that I may end my rhyme?
As with all loves, all lovers, that is time.

<u>The Folsom Place Revisited</u>
North of a farmhouse I once knew
a clump of Persian lilacs grew;

southward, a honey locust tree
shaded a pile of sand and me;

northeast, a roost for Leghorn hens;
southeast, the Poland Chinas' pens;

close by the shed where pigs got born
a red slat crib for golden corn;

dawnward, the barn where Daisy's calf
licked my nose and made me laugh.

I still see where the windmill rose,
where clotheslines wore their Monday clothes,

where Violets grew, where one small toad
lived in the ditch beside the road.

The road still passes-graveled now.
All else was buried by someone's plow.

Who had such need for beans, I wonder,
to burn and turn my childhood under?

# Chapter Twenty
# This Life

Fr. Frahm said repeatedly that life was a chancy thing. It is fundamentally unfair, extraordinarily brutal, and quite frequently, unbearable. It is also beautiful, mysterious, and supremely holy. Life is a reflection of God, and God must contain all truths, beautiful and otherwise.

According to Fr. Frahm, our lives are based largely on illusion. We participate in an individual and collective illusion which suggests that we are separate from one another and from God. We accept this illusion so completely that we never stop to consider the idea that it may not be real. We embrace the ideas of "I" and "You" so tightly that we prevent ourselves from ever seeing and feeling a sense of true connection with others, life and ultimately with God.

Fr. Frahm wanted us to stop and consider this idea. He wanted you to find the "I" inside but he did not want you to stop there. This, he suggested, is only the beginning. The real treasure, the gift that we are given by the divine, is our return to Him/Her. If we, out of choice, put aside the "I," we can rejoin the divine just as a river rejoins the sea. We can flow into the infinite, where we lose our illusions forever. This is home.

This process of returning home has to start in the struggles of your everyday life. For most of us, outside our acceptance of "I - You" distinction, the most significant mistake we make is to always pursue the positive and avoid the negative. Fr. Frahm taught that a wise man will never marry either the good or the bad side of life. To desire or expect one or the other of these will only bring you unhappiness. He was quite clear with those around him that it was our desire for and expectations for a life that is all good and all positive that causes us grief. We want everything to be good, and in a very childlike way, we expect it to be so. When it doesn't work out this way, we are shaken by an unpredictable and brutish world. The child emerges and feels betrayed by life and ultimately, by it's creator. Once we have been betrayed, we become angry, and we use this anger on ourselves, our world and our God.

In spite of this orientation, Fr. Frahm was not a nihilist or a 'nothing matters" person. In fact, he was quite the opposite. He taught that we need to live without expectations or desire for any particular outcome or experience. One should meet each day with acceptance and love for whatever comes, no matter how it is labeled or perceived. The ability to live with our day-to-day experience, without the need to change it, oppose it, control it, or escape it, was, for Fr. Frahm, the definition of well-being.

In the present moment, no matter what your circumstances, your heart can be filled with God. If you achieve this, there is no need to desire anything more than what you have. If you exist in the present moment, there is no need for yesterday or tomorrow, there is no need for good or bad. There is only God, right now. Here is an example from Plains Songs.

<u>Watercourse</u>
Does the drop of water
ever fret, I wonder,
how it finds the river?

Or the river hurry,
nagged by doubt to worry
it might not reach the sea?

When called upon to share
its vapors with the air,
does any ocean care?

Or skies become the less
should clouds in them address
some arid land's distress?

I, made mostly of water,
do ask about the matter.

Fr. Frahm amazed me with his ability to leave God free to run the universe as He/She saw fit. He had every reason to abandon God or try to control Him. He never did. When he was younger, he engaged in any one or more of these options, but by the time I knew him he possessed a profound acceptance and love for whatever it was that came that day. In the following poems from Summers Lease he talked about how he did it.

<u>Hope</u>
Hope, as her sister virtue Love, is blind,
and Faith alone of all the scriptured three
discerns a pathway often ill-defined
through eyes that, filled with tears, but dimly see.

But Hope can hear what Faith may but presume
and Love, overwhelmed, will scarcely dare believe:
echoes of music from that largest room
prepared for each, that all as a gift receive.
Yet Hope is mute; while Faith has powers of speech
to shout of joys beyond imagining
or whisper dreams outside a mortal's reach,
still Hope waits on, for Love fulfilled can sing.
    Take Faith or Love, I'll carry on and cope;
    But leave me. Lord, my silent, sightless Hope.

<u>To Jesus On The Rood XIV</u>
I sometimes think I have, great Son of God,
an ever so feeble grasp of who you are.
Yet, knowing but ill one tiny piece of sod,
how shall I think to comprehend a star?
Birth, life and death-these, too, are mystery
which, though much probed, still dazzles curious eyes;
add to that list this image of God's, this me,
and any else who goes in human guise.
Jesus, through whom all things that are were made-
subsisting through your constant agency-
should I now marvel much, or be afraid,
to find all sapped by the roots of your sweet tree?
    This is enough for me to understand:
    my world, all worlds, cradled in your pierced hand.


**Exercises:** No...No More. You have everything you need. Work to love always and in all ways. Bring awareness to your life through practice. Every day and at every opportunity...breathe. Remember there is no wrong way to be who you are.


## Stories

On a beautiful summer day Fr. Frahm and I were driving to lunch. We passed by a group of runners on their lunch time work out. He looked at me and asked if I had ever seen a runner smile. I thought for a moment and said I didn't think I had. He said "It is because we have mistaken wellness for well-being. What we all want desperately is to feel whole within ourselves. The problem is that many of us are trying to fill emptiness inside us by creating a better looking and a better feeling outside. We are all runners chasing something we can't catch." I asked him what he thought we should do. He replied, "To begin with we need to stop running once in awhile and just sit."

......................................................................

Fr. Frahm had little time for ideology and symbols. One day, I heard him say, "In a war of ideologies, it is the people who are the casualties. People will often kill for money and power; the most ruthless will kill for their ideas."

......................................................................

We were at lunch with a group of people. A conversation was going on about the merits of doing service for others. Fr. Frahm was not opposed to this, but was always careful about the idea. After one gentleman finished speaking, Fr. Frahm said, "Yes, it sounds like you were doing good unto others, WHETHER OTHERS WANTED GOOD DONE UNTO THEM OR NOT." Anyone who suggests that you are not acceptable the way you are needs to be watched. They may be trying to change you into what they think you should be.

......................................................................

A friend of Fr. Frahm's came to him for confession. After hearing his confession, (which I did not hear), we had tea. The conversation continued. The man expressed the belief that what he had done had changed him forever. Fr. Frahm spoke with him alone again. Soon, the individual left. I asked Fr. Frahm if this man was going to be alright. He said, "yes." Then he turned and told me to remember that people will always believe that they pay for wisdom with the coin of their innocence. Sometimes, you have to show them that the purse is never really empty.

......................................................................

My time with Fr. Frahm was all too brief. He loved me and allowed me the time to discover how to love. In the process of loving and being loved, I discovered who I was. In the years we spent together, he gave me what I now consider to be the secret to life, although I am, at present, not entirely sure what the secret means or how always to implement it, I think it's appropriate if I end this section by sharing the secret with you.

Fr. Frahm would say, "God begins and ends in mystery. Other people are now, and will always be, a mystery. Ultimately I am a mystery to myself. The secret to life is to learn to love the mystery. If you are unsure how to do this, I suggest that every day you practice loving the mystery that is yourself."

# Afterward

I have often heard people talk of God's grace during my life. Some spoke of having God's grace. Others spoke of wanting it. For me, these discussions were lofty and ambiguous because I did not have any idea of what grace was, let alone God's grace. More interestingly, I had never given the question much thought until a late afternoon in August when my wife and I were driving to Sioux City to attend Fr. Frahm's memorial service.

As a result of losing my father at 15, my relationship with him was forever frozen at that age. I had only just entered that period of my life were I was to develop a relationship with him as an adult. All boys need an ongoing relationship with an adult male who will allow them to be seen as men and have that manhood acknowledged and invited into the world. The relationship with my father was to be the map that sustained me as I went out to find who I would become. In one cold October moment that map disappeared. With it went my identity and my future. I was frozen, forever 15 years old.

For more than 10 years, I lived in that state of exile. I tried to be many things I thought I was or should be, only to find that I was none of them. By my mid-20's I was beginning to suspect that I was nothing, that I could never fill the hole in my heart. Then I met a strange old man who reached out to me and saved me from the wilderness. He went on to teach me about who I was. He gave me back my ability to love. Although, I am by all accounts a grown man, Fr. Frahm, or Gary, as I called him, had become the father I had desperately needed. Now, he was gone.

It was three o'clock and my wife was driving me to a memorial service where I was supposed to speak. I had no idea what I would say. If I managed to think of something to say, I doubted that I would be able to do it without collapsing into tears. What was I to say about someone who had given me just, everything? We drove south. I stared at a blank legal pad trying to jot down a few notes that I hoped would sustain me as I tried to say something. Nothing came. I finally just stared out the window.

I started thinking about the only thing that was holding me together at that moment. I had spent most of my daylight hours in the week prior sitting by Gary's bedside watching him slowly slip inside himself toward a place I could not follow. He became less aware, then less conscious until, in the last day or so, he rarely if ever opened his eyes.

I spoke to the doctor on the afternoon of his last day. She told me the end was very close. I returned to his room and found him alone. I leaned toward his head, stroked the hair above a gaunt face and whispered "It's almost over now, I think I should tell you goodbye." He took a long breath and held it. For a moment I thought that he was going to die right there. After a few seconds his eyes opened and he looked up at me. I gazed at the life I had known only a week before as it spread across his face.

He postponed his journey and crossed a great distance for me in that one breath. I knew he would not be able to stay long, even if he wanted to, which I knew he didn't. All I could do was smile, and say "I love you." He smiled back and whispered the thing he knew I would need most, "You are a good person, and you always have been." I scooped him into my arms and cried into his shoulder. When I lifted myself up to look at him again the life I knew was gone.

Sitting in the car, it struck me. I had, for the last 10 years, lived in the grace that Gary had offered me. To be his friend was to live in the presence of love all the time. This love was tangible, ever present, and there were never any strings attached. I lived in his grace because I always knew his love was there. Grace is the place you are when you know that love is all there is.

Yesterday does not exist, tomorrow is unimportant, there is only love right now. Gary loved me as a father, a teacher and a critic but most importantly he loved me as a friend. This is a love that sustained me when I had been hurt or I had hurt myself, and the universe made no sense at all. Because of his love for me, I lived in a state of grace where I could love myself in the same way he loved me.

Grace is a choice. It is a way of existing in which you are connected with the one who extended that grace, the universe that contains it and ultimately, with the God at the center of the whole thing. Of course, I have to choose to accept this grace. And honestly, sometimes I don't. But when I want it, I can live in the grace Gary offered me when he was alive, and still offers me each day, even though he's gone. When I reside within this grace I am my real self, creative, rebellious and loving. Everything is easier. I see my way clearly. But grace is also something much more subtle and important.

The final teaching I received from Gary that August afternoon was that grace is what moves two human souls toward one another and at the same time toward God. The grace he offered was a demonstration, a lesson about the eternal relationship I have with God even when I don't see it. I learned that I live in God's grace right now as surely as I live in the grace Gary offered. And most importantly, I can experience it right now.

The human soul is always trying to find its way back to God. It will look everywhere for God and for the promise of God. Some of the places we go are good for us and some are not. But the soul never stops searching. Ultimately, we hear a rumor that God resides in our own heart. If we are lucky, we find some-one, an old one, who will offer us the grace necessary to take us there.

Whenever I think of Gary or what he taught me, I live in grace. I make every effort to be in his grace each day. It opens me up, it breaks my heart. It destroys the me that obscures what is real in life. With "me" gone, I'm free.

What can I say to you (the reader) that will adequately end this experience for both of us? Nothing would be sufficient so I will not even try. As for me, I will continue to live in grace and let it move me toward the larger mystery I so badly want to touch.


Gary, I know you were a poem written by God. I miss you.

# Biography of Fr. Frahm

Born in Omaha, September 26, 1937, Fr. Gary Frahm spent his childhood years in Saunders County, Nebraska. He received a Bachelor of Arts degree from Westmar College, Le Mars, Iowa, in 1959. Fr. Frahm graduated from the Episcopal Theological School, Cambridge, Massachusetts in 1962 (S.T.B.) and was ordered to the Diaconate of the Episcopal Church in that year. He was ordained to the Priesthood in 1963. From the time of his ordination until his retirement in 1983, he served churches in communities throughout Iowa, among them Decorah, Carroll, Fairfield, Oskaloosa and Sioux City. After his retirement in 1983, he lived the rest of his life in Sioux City. He died in August of 2002.

# About the Author

Daniel Burow is a writer, psychologist and teacher who has studied for over a decade with masters in the Christian, Hindu and Taoist sacred traditions. His clinical practice is focused on adult and geriatric psychotherapy and hypnotherapy, working extensively with psychological trauma and chronic illness, on existential and spiritual problems, and the process of death and dying. He is also a management consultant for progressive and socially responsible health care clinics and programs. He lives with his family in Sioux Falls, South Dakota.

Feel free to contact Daniel Burow at anotherkindoffreedom@gmail.com.

# Bibliography


1. K. Barker & D. Burdick, Eds. <u>The NIV Study Bible,</u> New International Version
Zondervan Publishing, Michigan, 1985.
2. Burow, D. <u>Silence, Mystery and Just Plains Foolishness.</u> Unpublished Manuscript 2002.
3. Burow, Daniel. <u>Personal papers and correspondence.</u>
4. de Mello, Anthony, S.J. <u>The Heart Of The Enlightened.</u> Doubleday, NY. 1989.
5. Donne, J. <u>The Complete English Poems.</u> Penguin, London. 1971.
6. Frahm, G. J., <u>Summer's Lease.</u> Dordt College Press, Sioux Center, IA. 1989
7. Frahm, G. J., <u>Plains Songs.</u> Morningside College Press, Sioux City, IA. 2002.
8. Ladinsky, D. (Trans) <u>Hafiz: The Gift.</u> Compass, New York. 1999.
9. Lewis, C.S., <u>Poems.</u> HBJ, NY. 1997.
10. Maharishi, R. <u>The Spiritual Teachings of Ramana Maharishi,</u> Shambala, Berkely. 1972
11. Merton, T. (1964). (Ed.). <u>Gandi on non-violence: A selection from the writings of Mahatma Gandi.</u> New York: New Directions.
12. Mitchell, S., <u>Parables and Portraits.</u> Harper, NY. 1991
13. Mitchell, S., <u>Tao Te Ching.</u> Harper, NY. 1991.